RENEWING ✠ WORSHIP

Holy Communion

and Related Rites

Evangelical Lutheran Church in America
Published by Augsburg Fortress

RENEWING WORSHIP 6
Holy Communion and Related Rites

Also available:
Renewing Worship Liturgies (Pew Edition)
AFP 0-8066-7025-8
Renewing Worship Liturgies (Accompaniment Edition)
AFP 0-8066-7026-6

This resource has been prepared by the Evangelical Lutheran Church in America for provisional use.

The paper used in this publication meets the minimum requirements of American National Standard for Information Sciences—Permanence of Paper for Printed Library Materials, ANSI Z329.48-1984.

Manufactured in the U.S.A. ISBN 0-8066-7006-1

08 07 06 05 04   1   2   3   4   5

Contents

Preface

In the years since the publication of *Lutheran Book of Worship* in 1978, the pace of change both within the church and beyond has quickened. The past three decades have seen not only a growing ecumenical consensus but also a deepened focus on the church's mission to the world. The church has embraced broadened understandings of culture, increasing musical diversity, changes in the usage of language, a renewed understanding of the central pattern of Christian worship, and an explosion of electronic media and technologies. These shifts have had a profound effect on the weekly assembly gathered around word and sacrament. The present situation calls for a renewal of worship and of common resources for worship, a renewal grounded in the treasures of the church's history while open to the possibilities of the future.

Renewing Worship is a response to these emerging changes in the life of the church and the world. Renewing Worship includes a series of provisional resources intended to provide worship leaders with a range of proposed strategies and materials that address the various liturgical and musical needs of the church. These resources are offered to assist the renewal of corporate worship in a variety of settings, especially among Lutheran churches, in anticipation of the next generation of primary worship resources.

Published beginning in 2001, this series includes hymns and songs (newly written or discovered as well as new approaches to common texts and tunes), liturgical texts and music for weekly and seasonal use, occasional rites (such as marriage, healing, and funeral), resources for daily prayer (morning prayer, evening prayer, and prayer at the close of the day), psalms and canticles, prayers and lectionary texts, and other supporting materials. Over the course of several years, worship leaders will have the opportunity to obtain and evaluate a wide range of Renewing Worship resources both in traditional print format and in electronic form delivered via the Internet (www.renewingworship.org).

These published resources, however, are only one component of the Renewing Worship multiyear plan led by the Evangelical Lutheran Church in America (ELCA) as it enters the next generation of its worship life. Endorsed by the ELCA Church Council and carried out in partnership by the ELCA Division for Congregational Ministries and the Publishing House of the ELCA (Augsburg Fortress), this plan for worship renewal includes five components. The first phase (2001–2002) is a consultative process intended to develop principles for language, music, preaching, and worship space. Related to the ELCA's statement on sacramental practices, *The Use of the Means of Grace*, the outcome of the 2001–2002 consultative process has been published as *Principles for Worship*. These principles are intended to undergird future worship resource development and encourage congregational study, response, and practice.

The second phase (2001–2005) includes a series of editorial teams that collect, develop, and revise worship materials for provisional use. The liturgical and musical resource proposals that emerge from the editorial teams are being published during the third phase of this plan (also in 2001–2005) as trial-use resources in the Renewing Worship series, including the present volume, *Holy Communion and Related Rites*. These materials include proposals for newly developed, ecumenically shared, or recently revised texts, rites, and music. Crucial to this phase will be careful evaluation and response by congregations and worship leaders based on these proposed strategies and provisional materials.

The fourth phase of the plan includes regional conferences for conversation, resource introduction and evaluation, and congregational feedback. The final phase of the process (2005 and beyond) envisions the drafting of a comprehensive proposal for new primary worship resources designed to succeed *Lutheran Book of Worship*.

As the plan progresses, the shape and parameters of that proposal will continue to unfold. The goal, however, will remain constant: renewing the worship of God in the church as it carries out Christ's mission in a new day.

Introduction

Holy Communion and Related Rites, the sixth resource in the Renewing Worship series, focuses on the patterns of the people of God as they gather in the primary weekly assembly to worship God in the proclamation of the word and the celebration of the sacraments.[1] In addition to the presentation of an annotated shape of the rite and a body of core as well as supplemental texts, this resource includes samples of newly composed music for the rite. Two examples of communion liturgies incorporate settings by different composers of acclamations for the word and meal portions. Other service music options are presented in a separate section, from which worship planners can select appropriate choices. Several outlined examples illustrate how different options can shape the liturgy for particular occasions. Finally, this resource includes a Service of Word and Thanksgiving for use on those occasions when the Lord's supper is not included in the liturgy.

It is important to emphasize that this volume is not a complete collection of the texts and liturgical music to be proposed for the worship resources that will replace *Lutheran Book of Worship (LBW).* This provisional volume includes mostly a sampling of new materials offered for testing and evaluation. Longer-term core resources will include also some materials carried over from current usage. Feedback from congregations about existing materials and response to these newly proposed materials will help determine the balance between "new" and "old" that will be recommended for use.

An essential foundation for all Renewing Worship resources is *The Use of the Means of Grace,* the statement on the practice of word and sacrament adopted for guidance and practice by the Evangelical Lutheran Church in America in 1997.[2] Some highlights from that statement are noted in the following introduction, but the statement's intent and spirit are best captured by a careful study of the original. In addition to *The Use of the Means of Grace,* the churchwide consultative work that resulted in the 2002 release of *Principles for Worship* has provided guidance and support for the work on these provisional materials.[3]

A PRIMARY DAY

"Sunday, the day of Christ's resurrection and of the appearances to the disciples by the crucified and risen Christ, is the primary day on which Christians gather to worship."[4] Christians may, of course, gather for the liturgy of word and sacrament on other days of the week, particularly on festival days. By their exceptional character, though, these occasions may serve to underscore the norm, that "Sunday is the principal festival day of Christians."[5] The materials in this provisional resource are prepared first and foremost for the primary Sunday gathering of the Christian community.

---

[1] Constitution, Bylaws, and Continuing Resolutions of the Evangelical Lutheran Church in America, 1995, 4.02.
[2] *The Use of the Means of Grace: A Statement on the Practice of Word and Sacrament* (Chicago: Evangelical Lutheran Church in America, 1997).
[3] *Principles for Worship,* Renewing Worship, vol. 2 (Minneapolis: Augsburg Fortress, 2002).
[4] *The Use of the Means of Grace,* principle 6.
[5] *The Use of the Means of Grace,* application 6A.

A PRIMARY PATTERN FOR UNITY

The fundamental pattern of this liturgy of word and sacrament is grounded in the Bible, the Lutheran confessions, and the continuing witness of the church across time and space. Centered in the proclamation of the word and the sharing of the eucharistic meal, the pattern includes also the gathering of the worshiping community and the sending of the people to continue the mission of God. The materials in this provisional resource reflect a commitment to this common, ecumenical pattern of gathering, word, meal, and sending.

A PRIMARY PRINCIPLE OF FLEXIBILITY

"Freedom and flexibility in worship is a Lutheran inheritance, and there is room for ample variety in ceremony, music, and liturgical form. Having considered their resources and their customs, congregations will find their own balance between fully using the ritual and musical possibilities of the liturgy, and a more modest practice."[6] Recognizing the increasing diversity of local contexts and customs among Lutherans, the materials in this provisional resource encourage this principle of flexibility within the common pattern of the rite, while acknowledging that no single resource, provisional or more permanent, can contain or accommodate every possible variation.

A PRIMARY OPENNESS TO ECUMENICAL PARTNERS

The proper focus of the Renewing Worship process is to bring renewal to Lutheran worship. Lutherans, however, have much in common with other Christian traditions, and especially those with whom they are in formal partnership. An openness to ecumenical companions is evident in this resource, in part through the use of texts agreed upon by the English Language Liturgical Consultation, in which the Evangelical Lutheran Church in America actively participates. Since the release of these texts in 1988, a growing number of church bodies have accepted them for use, including several of the churches with which the ELCA is in a full communion relationship. Additionally, three of the eucharistic prayers provided are drawn from resources of the Presbyterian Church (U.S.A.), the Episcopal Church, and the United Church of Canada.

A PRIMARY UNDERSTANDING OF WORSHIP LEADERSHIP

One of the expressed goals of *Lutheran Book of Worship* was "to involve lay persons as assisting ministers who share the leadership of corporate worship."[7] *The Use of the Means of Grace* continues this trajectory by identifying various roles through which the baptized carry out their responsibility for the liturgy of word and sacrament, such as readers, interpreters, cantors, leaders of prayer, musicians, servers of communion, acolytes, those who prepare for the meal, and those who offer hospitality.[8] The materials in this provisional resource continue and expand upon this emphasis that "The liturgy is the celebration of all who gather. Together with the pastor who presides, the entire congregation is involved."[9]

---

[6] *Lutheran Book of Worship,* Introduction, 8.
[7] *Lutheran Book of Worship,* Introduction, 8.
[8] *The Use of the Means of* Grace, applications 8A and 8B, principle 41.
[9] *Lutheran Book of Worship* Ministers Edition, 25, quoted in *The Use of the Means of Grace,* background 41B.

A PRIMARY PLACE FOR SINGING

The singing of hymns and liturgical songs is another treasured element of the Lutheran inheritance in worship. For over one hundred years most service books used by Lutherans in North America and the Caribbean have included a collection of hymns in addition to forms of the liturgy in which liturgical song is embedded. The materials prepared for this provisional resource carry forward this central emphasis on assembly singing. At the same time, an effort is made here to test some new melodies for singing the liturgy that can at least partially bridge the many different musical styles presently in use in congregations. In addition, continuing the pattern provided in *With One Voice,* this resource and its accompanying full score companion offer a broader range of service music than was available in previous primary worship books.

A PRIMARY ORIENTATION TOWARD MISSION

The Use of the Means of Grace emphasizes the integral relationship of the worship of God and the mission of God. The proclamation of God's word and the celebration of the sacraments *are* the mission of God, set in the midst of the world for the life of the world. At the same time, through these means of grace God acts to empower the church for the ongoing mission of witness, service, and striving for justice.[10] The materials prepared for this provisional resource aim to make this missional intention and focus clear, seeking to make the words and songs of the liturgy both accessible and durable, extending hospitality to the stranger while nourishing the established community. A further aspect of this outward-focused emphasis is the use of texts that expand beyond traditional male- and hierarchically-oriented language, in order that all may better recognize God's generous welcome.

HOLY COMMUNION AND RELATED RITES—GUIDE TO THIS RESOURCE

Most of this resource is devoted to presenting provisional materials for the church's primary gathering around word and table. These materials include the following:

▶ *Shape of the Rite:* a brief description of the common pattern for worship and an annotated outline of the elements of the rite. Each element is accompanied by a brief description that suggests the dialogical nature of worship: the gracious gifts of God and the grateful response of God's people.

▶ *Text of the Rite:* a text-only presentation of the core materials proposed for the communion liturgy, so that these can be seen and evaluated apart from the musical settings of some of these texts.

▶ *Provisional Settings A and B:* presentations of the communion liturgy with music in place for the gospel and eucharistic acclamations. The acclamations offer examples of the new music commissioned from two composers for this resource. Each of these examples includes two models for giving thanks at table. One of these models provides

---

[10] *The Use of the Means of Grace,* principle 51, application 51B.

a eucharistic prayer, continuing the richness of this tradition from *Lutheran Book of Worship* and *Service Book and Hymnal*. The other model offers an abbreviated, yet still complete, sung version of the great thanksgiving.

▶ *Supplemental Materials:* a section of additional alternative texts for elements of the liturgy, in addition to the few that appear in the Text of the Rite. In particular, this section contains the initial thanksgivings (prefaces) for the church year and a fuller complement of thanksgivings at table (eucharistic prayers). (Additional seasonal texts and other propers will be included in *The Church's Year,* volume 8 in this series.)

▶ *Models for Shaping the Liturgy:* illustrations of ways in which the rite can be tailored by using various available options. As noted above, this resource continues and expands upon the flexibility offered in previous worship books, and this section demonstrates some ways in which those options may be arranged. The choices made in these illustrations are not intended to be normative or preferential; they are simply some ways in which the materials might be used on particular days or in various settings. Some of these models, with music in place, will be made available for download from the Renewing Worship Web site (www.renewingworship.org).

▶ *Additional Service Music:* settings of canticles and other portions of the liturgy, especially for the gathering and sending sections. Some of these canticles continue the musical settings offered in the provisional settings. Together with the other service music, these portions provide many opportunities to shape the liturgy for the day or assembly. The musical settings in this part of the resource are only a sample of some elements that can be used.

In addition to these materials for the communion liturgy, the resource includes an annotated outline and a rite for a Service of Word and Thanksgiving, described in more detail below.

HOLY COMMUNION: GATHERING

From one perspective, the act of gathering for worship may seem merely functional and preliminary. A body of people must assemble in a place in order for there to be an assembly. From another perspective, the gathering of the assembly is itself the activity of God: the Holy Spirit "calls, gathers, enlightens, and sanctifies" the church, according to the *Small Catechism.*[11] The Greek word for church, *ekklesia,* reinforces this image of the church as those who are called out and called together. Music has often played an important role in this action of bringing people from their scattered lives and forming them into one body for worship.

In this resource the proposal for the gathering rite includes several aspects that differ from the rite presented in *Lutheran Book of Worship*.

---

[11] *The Small Catechism,* the Third Article of the Apostles Creed.

- This proposal encourages an even greater sense of *flexibility* to the shape of the gathering rite. Although *LBW* moved in this direction by suggesting seasonal variations within the entrance rite, the increasing variety of contexts in which Lutherans worship calls for a greater openness to the ways in which congregations gather.

- This allowance for flexibility is especially noticeable in the suggestions for *gathering song,* the time of assembly singing that accompanies the gathering of the people.

- This proposal suggests a more intentional recognition that the gathering of the assembly normally begins with a *remembrance of baptism,* the place of entry into the Christian community. The remembrance may be made in the context of a brief corporate order for confession and forgiveness that may often make a more direct connection with baptism. Or, the remembrance may be more extended: a thanksgiving for baptism at the font, followed by a visible and tangible sign, such as sprinkling the assembly with water.

- This proposal *relocates the apostolic greeting* to a place just prior to the prayer of the day so that there is a single moment of greeting by the presiding minister and assembly in the gathering rite. Although other forms of the greeting are possible, the fullness and trinitarian shape of the words from 2 Corinthians recommend this form for regular use.

HOLY COMMUNION: WORD

In this resource the section of the liturgy in which the word of God is proclaimed and acclaimed follows essentially the same pattern presented in *Lutheran Book of Worship.* The rich treasury of the Bible continues to shine, with readings from the Old Testament (and psalms in response), apostolic letters and other New Testament writings, and the four gospels. At several points there are modest proposals for revision.

- Reflected in this proposal is the practice, common in many places, of the assembly responding to the first two readings with "Thanks be to God." Two *alternate forms of the reader's words* at the conclusion to the reading are offered.

- The *gospel acclamation* (formerly named the verse) is given greater prominence as one of the chief acclamations in the liturgy, along with "Holy, holy, holy" in the great thanksgiving. It is suggested that the assembly normally sing the alleluia at the beginning and end of the acclamation, with the verse of the day sung by a cantor or choir between the alleluias.

- The *slightly revised wording of the Apostles and Nicene creeds* reflects the broad ecumenical consensus represented by the work of the English Language Liturgical Consultation. The limited changes to the words are a response both to continuing developments in the English language as well as the need for a greater clarity and accuracy in translating the original Greek. For example, "and became truly human" replaces "and was made man," offering a more precise translation of the Greek *anthropos*, and recognizing that modern English usage no longer uses "man" as a generic term denoting "humanity."

▶ The suggested *pattern for prayers of intercession is modified* and includes the recommendation for regularly using a petition for the created world.

▶ The peace is a transitional moment in the liturgy, standing between the proclamation of the word and the eucharistic meal, although *LBW* offered an alternate placement after the Lord's Prayer. This proposal suggests that *the greeting's most natural place falls at the end of the word section*, a placement that also reflects one ancient tradition interpreting this greeting as a summation and commendation to the risen Christ of the preceding prayers of intercession. "Peace be with you all" is a more direct quotation of the words of the risen Christ to the apostles, including the understanding that the "you" is plural.

HOLY COMMUNION: MEAL

In this resource the proposed pattern for the liturgy of the meal carries forward the essential aspects of the rite in *LBW*. Several additional developments may be noted.

▶ The *actions prior to the great thanksgiving* are named intuitively and simply: "gathering of gifts" and "setting the table." The focus of these actions is the collection of gifts for those in need and the mission of the church, as well as the functional need to prepare the table for the meal. Titles that emphasize what the worshipers are offering to God may be misleading.

▶ This proposed rite suggests that the words of *an appropriate canticle or song*, sung by the assembly as the bread and wine and other gifts are brought to the table, are sufficient to interpret the action, making an additional prayer at the conclusion of this action optional. Again, an "offertory prayer" at this point may tend unhelpfully to shift the focus from God's actions for us to our contributions. If such a prayer is still desired, however, some options are presented among the supplemental texts.

▶ The proposed *pattern for the great thanksgiving* makes it clear that, whether brief or extended, the prayer indeed gives thanks for the gifts of God. A fuller form of the great thanksgiving, of which a larger collection of options is made available, includes a rich tracing of aspects of God's saving work, prays for the Holy Spirit, and offers more opportunities for the people to respond in song. A briefer form of the great thanksgiving nevertheless incorporates the initial words of thanksgiving (the preface) and the narrative of the Lord's supper with Jesus' words of promise and command. This range of possibilities reflects the continuing diversity among Lutheran traditions at this moment in the rite.

- *Both currently-used translations of the Lord's Prayer* are included in this proposal. Although in many places among Lutherans a generation has grown up knowing only the newer ecumenical version, it seems premature to propose that it be presented exclusively given the continuing widespread use of the older version.

- Options for an *invitation to the table* after the Lord's Prayer are proposed, connecting with ecumenical traditions and potentially expanding the role of the assisting minister.

- The flexible nature of singing at communion (communion song) in a variety of contexts is acknowledged. This proposal commends the *communing of the ministers at the conclusion* of the communion, accompanied by "Now, Lord, you let your servant go" or another appropriate concluding song. However, the alternative of communing the ministers first remains an option that has a long-standing tradition.

- The *communion prayer* (formerly post-communion prayer) is another transitional moment in the rite, giving thanks for the gifts of the meal and often also sending the assembly to continue the mission of God.

HOLY COMMUNION: SENDING

The sending rite is a brief but important part of the liturgy of holy communion. The words of the blessing and dismissal contain simple and direct reminders of God's presence as the assembly goes forth to serve in word and deed. Several additional developments may be noted here.

- The optional *sending of communion ministers*, provided for in *Occasional Services,* is here noted within the body of the rite. Thus the sending encompasses those who are not present in the assembly in addition to those who are.

- This proposal offers several additional *options for the words of the blessing*, providing for an expanded use of language and imagery for God in addition to traditional forms.

- It is suggested here that *the final words of the dismissal may be varied* to highlight various aspects of the assembly's witness and continuing mission in the world.

- This proposal also acknowledges the reality that in many places *song is a natural and customary part* of the sending.

SERVICE OF WORD AND THANKSGIVING

"According to the Apology of the Augsburg Confession, Lutheran congregations celebrate the Holy Communion every Sunday and festival. This confession remains the norm for our practice."[12] Although the frequency of weekly communion is increasing in the ELCA,

---

[12] *The Use of the Means of Grace*, principle 35.

even congregations that offer one service with communion every week may offer others without, and some congregations continue to offer communion less frequently than weekly.

The Service of Word and Thanksgiving in this resource proposes that one option for a non-eucharistic rite (other options include morning or evening prayer) parallel the fundamental pattern of the liturgy of word and meal. In place of the meal, however, a prayer of thanksgiving for the word of God is provided, which anticipates the fuller great thanksgiving of the communion liturgy. Since the gathering and word portions are shared with the holy communion liturgy, those parts are not reproduced here.

MUSIC FOR THE RITES

Included in this resource is a selected body of music commissioned for provisional use. The composers were asked to design melodies that could be accompanied in a range of musical genres, reflecting the diversity of musical accompaniments and styles in use among the churches. Provisional Setting A and Provisional Setting B in this resource include selections representing two different approaches to this musical assignment. A basic accompaniment for these materials is included in this resource. Accompaniments reflecting several other musical styles for many of the items in this resource are included in a supporting resource, *Renewing Worship Liturgies* (Accompaniment Edition), available from Augsburg Fortress (0806670266).

In addition to the newly commissioned music, a small sampling of service music from other sources is included to illustrate the breadth of possibilities for liturgical song.

USING THIS RESOURCE

This collection is intended for provisional use among congregations of the Evangelical Lutheran Church in America and beyond. Worship leaders are encouraged to consider a congregation's history and worship practices before introducing new materials.

Materials in this collection are designed for provisional use in worship. To facilitate trial use, the liturgies in this volume, along with additional service music, are available in an inexpensive congregational booklet, *Renewing Worship Liturgies*, which may be ordered from Augsburg Fortress (0806670258). Electronic files of selected materials are also available for download (www.renewingworship.org) and placement in congregational worship folders.

QUESTIONS OF COPYRIGHT

As a whole, the texts, music, and arrangement of materials in *Holy Communion and Related Rites* are covered under the copyright of this publication or are used here by arrangement with other publishers. Some individual items may be in the public domain. The acknowledgments section contains details about the sources.

Limited permission is granted to reproduce provisional texts and most of the provisional music for local congregational use until December 31, 2006. Information regarding this provision and the required copyright notice is included on the copyright page preceding the table of contents in this resource.

EVALUATION

An essential goal of Renewing Worship is the evaluation of strategies and content proposals by worshiping congregations and their leaders. Included in each printed volume as well as on the Web site (www.renewingworship.org) is an evaluation form that addresses the strategies employed in each volume of the series. Feedback received will help to shape the subsequent stages of the process toward new worship materials.

Holy Communion

Shape of the Rite
The Common Pattern for Worship in Word and Sacrament

At the heart of Christian worship is Jesus Christ, given by God through concrete and specific means. Through *baptism* God makes a people one body in Christ. In the *assembly* God gathers the people by the Holy Spirit. God's *word* is the message of Christ proclaimed in scripture reading, preaching, prayer, and singing. In the *meal* of communion God gives us Christ's very self in bread and wine. God then sends us to participate in Christ's mission in all the world.

The common shape of Christian worship has its roots in the scriptures. The story of the road to Emmaus in Luke 24 suggests a pattern that has been reflected in the church's worship since its earliest days. The story takes place on the first day of the week. A gathering of Jesus and two disciples focuses on the word, as the risen Christ explains the scriptures beginning with Moses and the prophets. In the meal that follows, the disciples recognize Jesus in the breaking of the bread. This recognition sends them out to share the news with others. A similar pattern is described in the book of Acts: the Christian community gathered on the first day of the week and devoted themselves to the apostles' teaching, to fellowship, to the breaking of bread, and to prayer.

Worship in word and sacrament continues to follow the simple pattern of gathering, word, meal, and sending, even though a variety of forms and styles may mark its practice. In fact, rich diversity of styles and openness to the ways of many peoples and nations can underscore how the central gifts of God unite us into one people in Christ. Worship in word and sacrament may be simple or it may be complex. But simplicity will not leave out the central things and complexity will not overshadow them.

Because worship takes place in contemporary settings, it is always current and new. At this very time, right now, the people meet the crucified and risen Christ, who baptizes into community, proclaims the word, feeds and nourishes with his body and blood, and sends the church to continue to be the body of Christ in the world.

Because worship is centered in word and sacrament, it always also extends beyond this time and place. Worship continues the story of all who have gone before us in faith, and so it always extends the wealth handed down from all those who have gathered and baptized, listened and shared the meal, and been sent to serve. Worship also connects the people of God across the world in the same word and sacrament and mission.

Worship in word and sacrament is God's gift to the church. The simple shape of the liturgy encourages local freedom to flower from a deep and faithful common ground. The life-giving gifts of God flow from the Holy Spirit who brings us to faith. They draw us into participation in the crucified and risen Christ. They show forth God's love for the world and make us part of that love. The central gifts of word and sacrament gather us into the very life of the triune God, the God who gives life to the world.

Shape of the Rite

GATHERING

The Holy Spirit gathers us in unity on the first day of the week, the day of Christ's resurrection.

Remembrance of Baptism
We remember our baptism . . .

   Confession and Forgiveness
. . . as we confess our need of God's mercy and hear the word of forgiveness,

   OR

   Thanksgiving for Baptism
. . . as we give thanks for God's mercy in the saving waters.

Gathering Song
We enter singing.

   Hymn, Song, Psalm
We draw from a rich treasury of song.

   AND/OR

   Kyrie
We pray for God's mercy to fill the church and the world.

   AND/OR

   Canticle of Praise
We sing the praise of God's glory revealed in Jesus Christ.

Greeting
The presiding minister and the assembly greet each other in the name of the triune God.

Prayer of the Day
The presiding minister leads the gathered assembly in prayer.

WORD

God speaks to us in scriptures read, sung, and preached.

First Reading
We listen to a scripture reading, most often from the Old Testament.

Psalm
We sing a psalm in response to the first reading.

Second Reading
We listen to a scripture reading, most often from the New Testament letters.

Gospel Acclamation
Singing, we welcome the gospel.

Gospel
We listen to a reading from one of the four gospels.

Sermon
We encounter the living word of God in the preaching.

Hymn of the Day
We proclaim the word of God in song.

Creed
With the baptized of every time and place we profess the faith.

Prayers of Intercession
We pray for the whole world.

Peace
At the close of the prayers, we greet one another with the peace of Christ.

Central elements of the liturgy are noted in bold letters; other elements support and reveal the essential shape of Christian worship.

MEAL

God feeds us with the presence of Jesus Christ.

Gathering of Gifts	*We gather gifts for those in need and the church's mission.*
Setting the Table	*Singing, we bring these gifts and set the table with bread and wine.*
Great Thanksgiving	*We thank and praise God, proclaiming Jesus Christ, praying for the Spirit, and concluding with the prayer Jesus taught.*
Dialog and Thanksgiving	*Opening our hearts to God, we begin the thanksgiving.*
Holy, Holy, Holy	*With the whole creation we join the angels' song.*
Thanksgiving	*Proclaiming and giving thanks for all God has done,*
Words of Institution	*we hear the promise of Jesus' gift through this meal.*
Remembrance and Acclamation	*We remember and acclaim the crucified and risen Christ.*
Prayer for the Holy Spirit	*We pray that the Holy Spirit come upon us and this meal.*
Final Praise and Amen	*We say Yes to this thanksgiving and to Christ among us.*
Lord's Prayer	*Empowered by the Spirit, we pray as Jesus taught us.*

OR

Dialog and Thanksgiving	*Opening our hearts to God, we begin the thanksgiving.*
Holy, Holy, Holy	*With the whole creation we join the angels' song.*
Words of Institution	*We hear the promise of Jesus' gift through this meal.*
Lord's Prayer	*Empowered by the Spirit, we pray as Jesus taught us.*
Communion	*Christ's body and blood nourishes faith, forgives sin, and forms us as living witnesses to God's promise of unity, justice, and peace.*
Communion Song	*We sing as the bread is broken, as the meal is shared, as the ministers commune.*
Communion Prayer	*Thanking God for these gifts, we ask God to send us in witness to the world.*

SENDING

God blesses us and sends us in mission to the world.

Sending of Communion Ministers	*We send ministers of communion to take the sacrament to the absent.*
Blessing	*We receive the blessing of the triune God.*
Sending Song	*Singing, we go out from the assembly as God's people in mission.*
Sending	*God sends us to live as Christ's body in the world.*

HOLY COMMUNION
Text of the Rite

GATHERING

Instrumental or vocal music or rehearsal of congregational song may take place while the assembly is gathering. An announcement of the day may be made, along with any brief comments about the day's worship.

The remembrance of baptism may precede gathering song. One of the following or another appropriate form may be used. If possible, the ministers (and the assembly) gather at the font.

I   REMEMBRANCE OF BAPTISM
    Confession and Forgiveness

All may make the sign of the cross in remembrance of baptism as the presiding minister begins:

A

Trusting in the word of life
given in baptism,
we are gathered in the name
of the Father, and of the ✝ Son,
and of the Holy Spirit.
Amen.

B

Blessed be God,
who gives us life with all of creation,
joins us to the saving death of ✝ Christ,
and raises us to new life by the Holy Spirit.
Blessed be the Holy Trinity.
Blessed be God forever.

The presiding minister may lead a prayer of preparation:
God of all mercy and consolation,
come to the aid of your people,
turning us from our sin to live for you alone.
Give us the power of your Holy Spirit
that we may confess our sins,
receive your forgiveness,
and grow into the fullness of your Son,
Jesus Christ our Lord.
Amen.

An assisting minister may invite the assembly into the confession:
God so loved the world
that while we were yet sinners
Jesus Christ was given to die for us.
Through the power of the Holy Spirit
God promises to heal us and forgive us.
Let us confess our sin
in the presence of God and of one another.

Silence is kept for reflection and self-examination.

The presiding minister leads a prayer of confession:

A

Gracious God,
have mercy on us.
In your compassion
forgive us our sins,
known and unknown,
things done and things left undone.
Uphold us by your Spirit
so that we may live and serve you
in newness of life,
to the honor and glory
of your holy name;
through Jesus Christ our Lord.
Amen.

B

Merciful God,
we have sinned against you
in thought, word, and deed,
and are not worthy
to be called your children.
Have mercy on us
and turn us from our sinful ways.
Bring us back to you
as those who once were dead
but now have life,
through our Savior Jesus Christ.
Amen.

The presiding minister announces God's forgiveness:

A

Almighty God looks upon us with mercy
and by water and the word joins us
to the saving death of Jesus Christ.
Through the Holy Spirit
God raises us with Christ to new life.
I therefore declare to you
the entire forgiveness of all your sins,
in the name of the Father,
and of the ✝ Son,
and of the Holy Spirit.
Amen.

B

Almighty God have mercy on you,
forgive you all your sins
through our Lord Jesus Christ,
strengthen you in all goodness,
and by the power of the Holy Spirit
keep you in eternal life.
Amen.

The liturgy may continue with gathering song.

II REMEMBRANCE OF BAPTISM
Thanksgiving for Baptism

All may make the sign of the cross in remembrance of baptism as the presiding minister begins:

A	B
Trusting in the word of life	Blessed be God,
given in baptism,	who gives us life with all of creation,
we are gathered in the name	joins us to the saving death of ☩ Christ,
of the Father, and of the ☩ Son,	and raises us to new life by the Holy Spirit.
and of the Holy Spirit.	Blessed be the Holy Trinity.
Amen.	**Blessed be God forever.**

The assisting minister invites the assembly into the remembrance of baptism:
When we were joined to Christ in the waters of baptism,
we were clothed with God's mercy and forgiveness.
Together let us remember our baptism.

Water may be poured into the font as the presiding minister gives thanks:
The Lord be with you.
And also with you.

Let us give thanks to the Lord our God.
It is right to give our thanks and praise.

We give you thanks, O God,
for in the beginning your Spirit brooded over the waters
and you created the world by your Word,
calling forth life in which you took delight.
You led Israel safely through the Red Sea into the land of promise,
and in the waters of the Jordan, you proclaimed Jesus your beloved one.
By water and the Spirit you adopted us as your daughters and sons,
making us heirs of the promise and servants of God.
Through this water remind us of our baptism.
Shower us with your Spirit,
that your forgiveness, grace, and love may be renewed in our lives.
To you be given honor and praise through Jesus Christ our Lord
in the unity of the Holy Spirit, now and forever.
Amen.

The water may be sprinkled over the people or they may be invited to use it to sign themselves with the cross. During this time gathering song may be sung. Hymns and songs related to baptism are especially appropriate.

The liturgy continues with the greeting and the prayer of the day.

GATHERING SONG

One or more of the following may be sung as the assembly gathers:

Hymn, Song, Psalm

Kyrie
When a Kyrie is sung, one of the following or another appropriate form may be used.

A

An assisting minister sings or speaks the invitations to prayer in this form of the Kyrie:

In peace, let us pray to the Lord.
Lord, have mercy.

For the peace from above,
and for our salvation,
let us pray to the Lord.
Lord, have mercy.

For the peace of the whole world,
for the well-being of the church of God,
and for the unity of all,
let us pray to the Lord.
Lord, have mercy.

For this holy house,
and for all who offer here their worship and praise,
let us pray to the Lord.
Lord, have mercy.

Help, save, comfort, and defend us, gracious Lord.
Amen.

B

Each sentence of this form of the Kyrie may be repeated one or more times:

Lord, have mercy.
Christ, have mercy.
Lord, have mercy.

C

Holy God,
holy and mighty,
holy and immortal,
have mercy on us.

Canticle of Praise

When a canticle of praise is sung, one of the following or another appropriate song may be used.

A

**Glory to God in the highest,
and peace to God's people on earth.
Lord God, heavenly King,
almighty God and Father,
    we worship you, we give you thanks,
    we praise you for your glory.
Lord Jesus Christ, only Son of the Father,
Lord God, Lamb of God,
you take away the sin of the world:
    have mercy on us;
you are seated at the right hand of the Father:
    receive our prayer.
For you alone are the Holy One,
you alone are the Lord,
you alone are the Most High,
    Jesus Christ,
    with the Holy Spirit,
    in the glory of God the Father. Amen.**

B

**This is the feast of victory for our God.
Alleluia.
Worthy is Christ, the Lamb who was slain,
whose blood set us free to be people of God.
Power, riches, wisdom, and strength,
and honor, blessing, and glory are his.
Sing with all the people of God,
and join in the hymn of all creation:
Blessing, honor, glory, and might
be to God and the Lamb forever. Amen.
For the Lamb who was slain has begun his reign.
Alleluia.**

GREETING

The presiding minister and the assembly greet each other:
The grace of our Lord Jesus Christ, the love of God,
and the communion of the Holy Spirit be with you all.
And also with you.

PRAYER OF THE DAY

The presiding minister prays the prayer of the day:
Let us pray.

A brief silence is kept before the prayer. After the prayer, the assembly responds:
Amen.

WORD

An announcement of the day may be made, along with any brief comments about the day's liturgy.

FIRST READING

An assisting minister proclaims the reading. The reading may be concluded:

A

Holy wisdom, holy word.
Thanks be to God.

B

The word of the Lord.
Thanks be to God.

PSALM   *The psalm for the day is sung.*

SECOND READING

An assisting minister proclaims the reading. The reading may be concluded:

A

Holy wisdom, holy word.
Thanks be to God.

B

The word of the Lord.
Thanks be to God.

GOSPEL ACCLAMATION

The assembly welcomes the gospel. The verse of the day or one of the following verses may be sung. The assembly or the choir may sing another alleluia, with or without verse, in place of this one.

A

Alleluia.
Lord, to whom shall we go?
You have the words of eternal life.
Alleluia.

B

Alleluia.
Your words are sweet to our taste,
sweeter than honey to our mouth.
Alleluia.

During Lent, the verse of the day, the following verse, or another seasonal acclamation may be sung.
Let your steadfast love come to us, O Lord;
save us as you promised, for we trust your word.

GOSPEL

The gospel is announced.
The holy gospel according to _____, the _____ chapter.
Glory to you, O Lord.

The gospel is proclaimed. The reading concludes:
The gospel of the Lord.
Praise to you, O Christ.

SERMON

Silence for reflection follows.

HYMN OF THE DAY

The assembly proclaims the word of God in song.

CREED

The assembly may profess the Nicene Creed or the Apostles Creed. The Nicene Creed is especially appropriate during Christmas, Easter, and on festival days; the Apostles Creed during Lent.

Nicene Creed

We believe in one God,
    the Father, the Almighty,
    maker of heaven and earth,
    of all that is, seen and unseen.

We believe in one Lord, Jesus Christ,
    the only Son of God,
    eternally begotten of the Father,
    God from God, Light from Light,
    true God from true God,
    begotten, not made,
    of one Being with the Father;
    through him all things were made.
    For us and for our salvation
        he came down from heaven,
        was incarnate of the Holy Spirit and the virgin Mary
        and became truly human.
        For our sake he was crucified under Pontius Pilate;
        he suffered death and was buried.
        On the third day he rose again
        in accordance with the scriptures;
        he ascended into heaven
        and is seated at the right hand of the Father.
        He will come again in glory to judge the living and the dead,
        and his kingdom will have no end.

We believe in the Holy Spirit, the Lord, the giver of life,
    who proceeds from the Father and the Son,*
    who with the Father and the Son is worshiped and glorified,
    who has spoken through the prophets.
    We believe in one holy catholic and apostolic church.
    We acknowledge one baptism for the forgiveness of sins.
    We look for the resurrection of the dead,
        and the life of the world to come. Amen.

*The phrase "and the Son" does not appear in the ancient, ecumenical version of the creed.

Apostles Creed

I believe in God, the Father almighty,
     creator of heaven and earth.

I believe in Jesus Christ, God's only Son, our Lord,
     who was conceived by the Holy Spirit,
     born of the virgin Mary,
     suffered under Pontius Pilate,
     was crucified, died, and was buried;
     he descended to the dead.
     On the third day he rose again;
     he ascended into heaven,
     he is seated at the right hand of the Father,
     and he will come to judge the living and the dead.

I believe in the Holy Spirit,
     the holy catholic church,
     the communion of saints,
     the forgiveness of sins,
     the resurrection of the body,
     and the life everlasting. Amen.

PRAYERS OF INTERCESSION

The prayers are crafted locally for each occasion using the following pattern or another appropriate form.

An assisting minister invites the assembly into prayer with these or similar words:
With the whole people of God in Christ Jesus, let us pray for the church,
those in need, and all of God's creation.

Prayers reflect the wideness of God's mercy for the whole world:
     for the church universal and its ministry;
     for creation and its right use;
     for peace and justice in the world, the nations and those in authority, the community and those who govern;
     for the poor and oppressed, the sick, the bereaved, the lonely, all who suffer in body, mind, or spirit;
     for the congregation, and special concerns.

The congregation may be invited to offer other petitions.

The assisting minister gives thanks for the faithful departed, especially for those who recently have died.

Each portion of the prayers concludes with these or similar words:

A	B
Lord, in your mercy,	Hear us, O God;
hear our prayer.	**your mercy is great.**

p. 56 ▶

The presiding minister concludes the prayers with these or similar words:

A
p. 56 ▶

Into your hands, gracious God, we commend all for whom we pray,
trusting in your mercy; through Jesus Christ our Savior.
Amen.

PEACE

The presiding minister and the assembly greet each other in the peace of the risen Christ:

A   B

Peace be with you all.   The peace of Christ be with you always.

And also with you.   **And also with you.**

The ministers and the assembly may greet one another with a gesture of Christ's peace, and may say these or similar words: Peace be with you.

MEAL

GATHERING OF GIFTS

Gifts may be gathered for those in need and for the mission of the church.

SETTING THE TABLE

The table of the eucharistic meal is prepared. "Let the vineyards be fruitful," "Create in me a clean heart," or another appropriate canticle, song, or hymn may be sung as bread, wine, money, and other gifts are brought to the table. A brief prayer acknowledging God as the source of every gift may follow.   pp. 56–57 ▶

GREAT THANKSGIVING

The presiding minister greets the assembly and invites all present to give thanks:

The Lord be with you.
And also with you.

Lift up your hearts.
We lift them to the Lord.

Let us give thanks to the Lord our God.
It is right to give our thanks and praise.

The presiding minister continues with an initial thanksgiving:

A (Sundays)   pp. 57–60 ▶

It is indeed right, our duty and our joy,
that we should at all times and in all places
give thanks and praise to you, almighty and merciful God,
through our Savior Jesus Christ;
who on this day overcame death and the grave,
and by his glorious resurrection opened to us the way of everlasting life.
And so, with all the choirs of angels,
with all the faithful of every time and every place,
we praise your name and join their unending hymn:
Holy, holy, holy Lord, God of power and might,
heaven and earth are full of your glory.
Hosanna in the highest.
Blessed is he who comes in the name of the Lord.
Hosanna in the highest.

The presiding minister continues the thanksgiving. One of the following or another appropriate form is used.

A pp. 61–71 ▶

You are indeed holy, almighty and merciful God.
You are most holy, and great is the majesty of your glory.
You so loved the world that you gave your only Son,
so that everyone who believes in him may not perish
but have eternal life.

Having come into the world to fulfill for us your holy will
and to accomplish all things for our salvation,
in the night in which he was betrayed,
our Lord Jesus took bread, and gave thanks;
broke it, and gave it to his disciples, saying:
Take and eat; this is my body, given for you.
Do this for the remembrance of me.

Again, after supper, he took the cup, gave thanks,
and gave it for all to drink, saying:
This cup is the new covenant in my blood,
shed for you and all people for the forgiveness of sin.
Do this for the remembrance of me.

Remembering, therefore, his salutary command,
his life-giving passion and death,
his glorious resurrection and ascension,
and the promise of his coming again,
we proclaim the mystery of faith.
Christ has died. Christ is risen. Christ will come again.

We give thanks to you, O Lord God Almighty,
not as we ought but as we are able;
we ask you mercifully to accept our praise and thanksgiving
and with your Word and Holy Spirit to bless us, your servants,
and these your own gifts of bread and wine,
so that we and all who share in the body and blood of Christ
may be filled with heavenly blessing and grace,
and, receiving the forgiveness of sin,
may be formed to live as your holy people
and be given our inheritance with all your saints.

To you, O God, Father, Son, and Holy Spirit,
be all honor and glory in your holy church, now and forever.
Amen.

The liturgy continues with the Lord's Prayer.

In the night in which he was betrayed,
our Lord Jesus took bread, and gave thanks;
broke it, and gave it to his disciples, saying:
Take and eat; this is my body, given for you.
Do this for the remembrance of me.

Again, after supper, he took the cup, gave thanks,
and gave it for all to drink, saying:
This cup is the new covenant in my blood,
shed for you and all people for the forgiveness of sin.
Do this for the remembrance of me.

Gathered into one by the Holy Spirit, let us pray as Jesus taught us:

A	B
Our Father in heaven,	**Our Father, who art in heaven,**
hallowed be your name,	**hallowed be thy name,**
your kingdom come,	**thy kingdom come,**
your will be done,	**thy will be done,**
on earth as in heaven.	**on earth as it is in heaven.**
Give us today our daily bread.	**Give us this day our daily bread;**
Forgive us our sins	**and forgive us our trespasses,**
as we forgive those	**as we forgive those**
who sin against us.	**who trespass against us;**
Save us from the time of trial	**and lead us not into temptation,**
and deliver us from evil.	**but deliver us from evil.**
For the kingdom, the power,	**For thine is the kingdom,**
and the glory are yours,	**and the power, and the glory,**
now and forever. Amen.	**forever and ever. Amen.**

COMMUNION

The presiding minister may raise the bread and cup and address the assembly with these or similar words:

A	B
Holy things for holy people.	The gifts of God for the people of God.
One is holy, one is Lord,	**Thanks be to God.**
Jesus Christ, to the glory of God.	

The assisting minister may conclude the invitation to the meal:
Taste and see that the Lord is good.

The bread may be broken for the communion.

When giving the bread and cup, the communion ministers say:
The body of Christ, given for you. The blood of Christ, shed for you.
and the communicant may respond, Amen.

The ministers commune either after or before the communion of the assembly.

Communion Song

Assembly song and other music may accompany the breaking of bread and the communion of the people, and may begin with the following:

Lamb of God, you take away the sin of the world; have mercy on us.
Lamb of God, you take away the sin of the world; have mercy on us.
Lamb of God, you take away the sin of the world; grant us peace.

At the conclusion of the communion, this or a similar song may be sung as the table is cleared:

Now, Lord, you let your servant go in peace:
your word has been fulfilled.
My own eyes have seen the salvation
which you have prepared in the sight of every people:
a light to reveal you to the nations
and the glory of your people Israel.
Glory to the Father, and to the Son, and to the Holy Spirit:
as it was in the beginning, is now, and will be forever. Amen.

Communion Prayer

An assisting minister leads one of these or a similar prayer:

Let us pray.

A

We give you thanks, almighty God,
that you have refreshed us
through the healing power
of this gift of life.
In your mercy
strengthen us through this gift
in faith toward you
and in fervent love toward one another;
for the sake of Jesus Christ our Lord.
Amen.

B

O God, we give you thanks
that you have set before us this feast,
the body and blood of your Son.
By your Spirit
strengthen us to serve all in want
and to give ourselves away
as bread for the hungry,
through Jesus Christ our Lord.
Amen.

SENDING

p. 72 ▶

SENDING OF COMMUNION MINISTERS

Communion ministers may be sent to bring the sacrament to those who are absent. The presiding minister may lead a prayer of sending.

Brief announcements related to the assembly's mission in the world may be made.

BLESSING

The presiding minister blesses the assembly with one of these or another appropriate blessing:

A	B	C
Holy Eternal Majesty,	The Lord bless you	Almighty God,
Holy Incarnate Word,	and keep you.	Father, ✝ Son,
Holy Abiding Spirit,	The Lord's face shine on	and Holy Spirit,
one God, ✝ bless you	you with grace and mercy.	bless you now and forever.
now and forever.	The Lord look upon you	**Amen.**
Amen.	with favor	
	and ✝ give you peace.	
	Amen.	

SENDING SONG

If "Now, Lord, you let your servant go" was not sung at the end of the communion, it may be sung here, or another sending song may be sung. The ministers may move to the door.

SENDING

The assisting minister sends the assembly forth with these or similar words:

A	B	C
Go in peace.	Go in peace.	Go in peace.
Share the good news.	Remember the poor.	Serve the Lord.
Thanks be to God.	**Thanks be to God.**	**Thanks be to God.**

HOLY COMMUNION
Provisional Setting A

GATHERING

Instrumental or vocal music or rehearsal of congregational song may take place while the assembly is gathering. An announcement of the day may be made, along with any brief comments about the day's worship.

The remembrance of baptism may precede gathering song. One of the following or another appropriate form may be used. If possible, the ministers (and the assembly) gather at the font.

I   REMEMBRANCE OF BAPTISM
     Confession and Forgiveness

All may make the sign of the cross in remembrance of baptism as the presiding minister begins:

A

Trusting in the word of life
given in baptism,
we are gathered in the name
of the Father, and of the ✝ Son,
and of the Holy Spirit.
Amen.

B

Blessed be God,
who gives us life with all of creation,
joins us to the saving death of ✝ Christ,
and raises us to new life by the Holy Spirit.
Blessed be the Holy Trinity.
Blessed be God forever.

The presiding minister may lead a prayer of preparation:

God of all mercy and consolation,
come to the aid of your people,
turning us from our sin to live for you alone.
Give us the power of your Holy Spirit
that we may confess our sins,
receive your forgiveness,
and grow into the fullness of your Son,
Jesus Christ our Lord.
Amen.

An assisting minister may invite the assembly into the confession:

God so loved the world
that while we were yet sinners
Jesus Christ was given to die for us.
Through the power of the Holy Spirit
God promises to heal us and forgive us.
Let us confess our sin
in the presence of God and of one another.

Silence is kept for reflection and self-examination.

A

Gracious God,
**have mercy on us.
In your compassion
forgive us our sins,
known and unknown,
things done and things left undone.
Uphold us by your Spirit
so that we may live and serve you
in newness of life,
to the honor and glory
of your holy name;
through Jesus Christ our Lord.
Amen.**

B

Merciful God,
**we have sinned against you
in thought, word, and deed,
and are not worthy
to be called your children.
Have mercy on us
and turn us from our sinful ways.
Bring us back to you
as those who once were dead
but now have life,
through our Savior Jesus Christ.
Amen.**

The presiding minister announces God's forgiveness:

A

Almighty God looks upon us with mercy
and by water and the word joins us
to the saving death of Jesus Christ.
Through the Holy Spirit
God raises us with Christ to new life.
I therefore declare to you
the entire forgiveness of all your sins,
in the name of the Father,
and of the ✝ Son,
and of the Holy Spirit.
Amen.

B

Almighty God have mercy on you,
forgive you all your sins
through our Lord Jesus Christ,
strengthen you in all goodness,
and by the power of the Holy Spirit
keep you in eternal life.
Amen.

The liturgy may continue with gathering song.

II REMEMBRANCE OF BAPTISM
Thanksgiving for Baptism

All may make the sign of the cross in remembrance of baptism as the presiding minister begins:

A	B
Trusting in the word of life	Blessed be God,
given in baptism,	who gives us life with all of creation,
we are gathered in the name	joins us to the saving death of ✢ Christ,
of the Father, and of the ✢ Son,	and raises us to new life by the Holy Spirit.
and of the Holy Spirit.	Blessed be the Holy Trinity.
Amen.	**Blessed be God forever.**

The assisting minister invites the assembly into the remembrance of baptism:
When we were joined to Christ in the waters of baptism,
we were clothed with God's mercy and forgiveness.
Together let us remember our baptism.

Water may be poured into the font as the presiding minister gives thanks:
The Lord be with you.
And also with you.

Let us give thanks to the Lord our God.
It is right to give our thanks and praise.

We give you thanks, O God,
for in the beginning your Spirit brooded over the waters
and you created the world by your Word,
calling forth life in which you took delight.
You led Israel safely through the Red Sea into the land of promise,
and in the waters of the Jordan, you proclaimed Jesus your beloved one.
By water and the Spirit you adopted us as your daughters and sons,
making us heirs of the promise and servants of God.
Through this water remind us of our baptism.
Shower us with your Spirit,
that your forgiveness, grace, and love may be renewed in our lives.
To you be given honor and praise through Jesus Christ our Lord
in the unity of the Holy Spirit, now and forever.
Amen.

The water may be sprinkled over the people or they may be invited to use it to sign themselves with the cross. During this time gathering song may be sung. Hymns and songs related to baptism are especially appropriate.

The liturgy continues with the greeting and the prayer of the day.

GATHERING SONG

One or more of the following may be sung as the assembly gathers:

Hymn, Song, Psalm

Kyrie

When a Kyrie is sung, one of the following or another appropriate form may be used.

A	Kyrie (Litany)	R312–R313 ▶
B	Kyrie (Threefold, Sixfold, or Ninefold)	R314–R317 ▶
C	Holy God (Trisagion)	R318–R319 ▶

Canticle of Praise

When a canticle of praise is sung, one of the following or another appropriate song may be used.

| A | Glory to God | R320–R322 ▶ |
| B | This is the feast | R323–R324 ▶ |

GREETING

The presiding minister and the assembly greet each other:

The grace of our Lord Jesus Christ, the love of God,
and the communion of the Holy Spirit be with you all.
And also with you.

PRAYER OF THE DAY

Let us pray.

A brief silence is kept. Then the presiding minister prays the prayer of the day. The assembly responds:
Amen.

WORD

An announcement of the day may be made, along with any brief comments about the day's liturgy.

FIRST READING

An assisting minister proclaims the reading. The reading may be concluded:

A	B
Holy wisdom, holy word.	The word of the Lord.
Thanks be to God.	**Thanks be to God.**

PSALM   *The psalm for the day is sung.*

SECOND READING

An assisting minister proclaims the reading. The reading may be concluded:

A	B
Holy wisdom, holy word.	The word of the Lord.
Thanks be to God.	**Thanks be to God.**

GOSPEL ACCLAMATION

The assembly welcomes the gospel. The verse of the day (R325) or the following verse may be sung. The assembly or the choir may sing another alleluia, with or without verse, in place of this one.

R301

R325–R329 ▶

Al - le - lu - ia, al - le - lu - ia.

Al - le - lu - ia, al - le - lu - ia.

Your words are sweet to our taste,

sweet-er than hon - ey to our mouth. Al - le -

lu - ia.

Al - le - lu - ia, al - le - lu - ia.

Al - le - lu - ia, al - le - lu - ia.

Let your stead-fast love come to us, O Lord;

save us as you prom-ised, for we trust your word.

GOSPEL

The gospel is announced.

The holy gospel according to _____, the _____ chapter.

Glory to you, O Lord.

The gospel is proclaimed. The reading concludes:

The gospel of the Lord.

Praise to you, O Christ.

SERMON

Silence for reflection follows.

HYMN OF THE DAY

The assembly proclaims the word of God in song.

CREED

The assembly may profess the Nicene Creed or the Apostles Creed. The Nicene Creed is especially appropriate during Christmas, Easter, and on festival days; the Apostles Creed during Lent.

Nicene Creed

We believe in one God,
    the Father, the Almighty,
    maker of heaven and earth,
    of all that is, seen and unseen.

We believe in one Lord, Jesus Christ,
    the only Son of God,
    eternally begotten of the Father,
    God from God, Light from Light,
    true God from true God,
    begotten, not made,
    of one Being with the Father;
    through him all things were made.
    For us and for our salvation
        he came down from heaven,
        was incarnate of the Holy Spirit and the virgin Mary
        and became truly human.
        For our sake he was crucified under Pontius Pilate;
        he suffered death and was buried.
        On the third day he rose again
        in accordance with the scriptures;
        he ascended into heaven
        and is seated at the right hand of the Father.
        He will come again in glory to judge the living and the dead,
        and his kingdom will have no end.

We believe in the Holy Spirit, the Lord, the giver of life,
    who proceeds from the Father and the Son,*
    who with the Father and the Son is worshiped and glorified,
    who has spoken through the prophets.
    We believe in one holy catholic and apostolic church.
    We acknowledge one baptism for the forgiveness of sins.
    We look for the resurrection of the dead,
        and the life of the world to come. Amen.

*The phrase "and the Son" does not appear in the ancient, ecumenical version of the creed.

Apostles Creed

I believe in God, the Father almighty,
  creator of heaven and earth.

I believe in Jesus Christ, God's only Son, our Lord,
  who was conceived by the Holy Spirit,
  born of the virgin Mary,
  suffered under Pontius Pilate,
  was crucified, died, and was buried;
  he descended to the dead.
  On the third day he rose again;
  he ascended into heaven,
  he is seated at the right hand of the Father,
  and he will come to judge the living and the dead.

I believe in the Holy Spirit,
  the holy catholic church,
  the communion of saints,
  the forgiveness of sins,
  the resurrection of the body,
  and the life everlasting. Amen.

PRAYERS OF INTERCESSION

The prayers are crafted locally for each occasion using the following pattern or another appropriate form.

An assisting minister invites the assembly into prayer with these or similar words:
With the whole people of God in Christ Jesus, let us pray for the church,
those in need, and all of God's creation.

Prayers reflect the wideness of God's mercy for the whole world:
  for the church universal and its ministry;
  for creation and its right use;
  for peace and justice in the world, the nations and those in authority, the community and those who govern;
  for the poor and oppressed, the sick, the bereaved, the lonely, all who suffer in body, mind, or spirit;
  for the congregation, and special concerns.

The congregation may be invited to offer other petitions.

The assisting minister gives thanks for the faithful departed, especially for those who recently have died.

Each portion of the prayers concludes with these or similar words:

A	B	p. 56, R331 ▸
Lord, in your mercy,	Hear us, O God;	
hear our prayer.	**your mercy is great.**	

The presiding minister concludes the prayers with these or similar words:

A   p. 56 ▸

Into your hands, gracious God, we commend all for whom we pray,
trusting in your mercy; through Jesus Christ our Savior.
Amen.

PEACE

The presiding minister and the assembly greet each other in the peace of the risen Christ:

A	B
Peace be with you all.	The peace of Christ be with you always.
And also with you.	**And also with you.**

The ministers and the assembly may greet one another with a gesture of Christ's peace, and may say these or similar words: Peace be with you.

MEAL

GATHERING OF GIFTS

Gifts may be gathered for those in need and for the mission of the church.

SETTING THE TABLE

The table of the eucharistic meal is prepared. "Let the vineyards be fruitful" (R332–R333), "Create in me a clean heart" (R334), or another appropriate canticle, song, or hymn may be sung as bread, wine, money, and other gifts are brought to the table. A brief prayer acknowledging God as the source of every gift may follow. *pp. 56–57* ▸

GREAT THANKSGIVING

The presiding minister greets the assembly and invites all present to give thanks:

The Lord be with you. **And al - so with you.**

Lift up your hearts. **We lift them to the Lord.**

Let us give thanks to the Lord our God.

It is right to give our thanks and praise.

A (Sundays)

pp. 57–60 ▶

It is indeed right, our du - ty and our joy, that we should at all times and

in all places give thanks and praise to you, al - mighty and merciful God,

through our Sav - ior Je - sus Christ; who on this day overcame

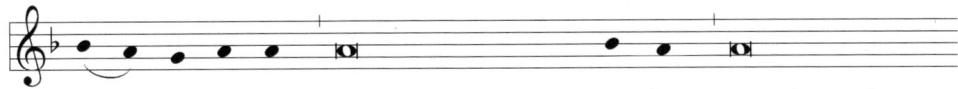

death and the grave, and by his glorious resur - rec - tion opened to us the way

of ev - er - last - ing life. And so, with all the choirs of an - gels,

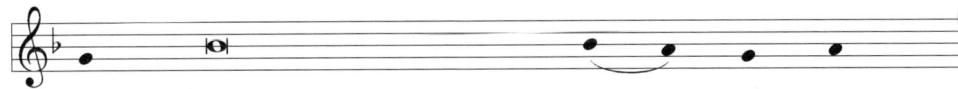

with all the faithful of every time and ev - 'ry place,

we praise your name and join their un - end - ing hymn:

*Sing either note

ho - san - na   in the high - est.

Blessed is   he   who comes in the name of the   Lord.

Ho - san - na   in the high - est,   ho -

san - na   in the high - est.

The presiding minister continues the thanksgiving. One of the following or another appropriate form is used.

A pp. 61–71 ▶

You are indeed holy, almighty and merciful God.
You are most holy, and great is the majesty of your glory.
You so loved the world that you gave your only Son,
so that everyone who believes in him may not perish
but have eternal life.

Having come into the world to fulfill for us your holy will
and to accomplish all things for our salvation,
in the night in which he was betrayed,
our Lord Jesus took bread, and gave thanks;
broke it, and gave it to his disciples, saying:
Take and eat; this is my body, given for you.
Do this for the remembrance of me.

Again, after supper, he took the cup, gave thanks,
and gave it for all to drink, saying:
This cup is the new covenant in my blood,
shed for you and all people for the forgiveness of sin.
Do this for the remembrance of me.

Remembering, therefore, his salutary command,
his life-giving passion and death,
his glorious resurrection and ascension,
and the promise of his coming again,
we proclaim the mystery of faith.

R304 R336, R339 ▶

Christ has died. Christ is ris - en.

Christ will come a - gain.

We give thanks to you, O Lord God Almighty,

not as we ought but as we are able;

we ask you mercifully to accept our praise and thanksgiving

and with your Word and Holy Spirit to bless us, your servants,

and these your own gifts of bread and wine,

so that we and all who share in the body and blood of Christ

may be filled with heavenly blessing and grace,

and, receiving the forgiveness of sin,

may be formed to live as your holy people

and be given our inheritance with all your saints.

To you, O God, Father, Son, and Holy Spirit,

be all honor and glory in your holy church, now and forever.

R305

R337, R340 ▶

The liturgy continues with the Lord's Prayer on p. 35.

B

In the night in which he was be-trayed, our Lord Je-sus

took bread, and gave thanks; broke it, and gave it to

his dis-ci-ples, say-ing: Take and eat; this is my bod-y,

giv-en for you. Do this for the re-mem-brance of me.

A-gain, after supper, he took the cup, gave thanks, and gave it for all to drink,

say-ing: This cup is the new covenant in my blood, shed for you and all people

for the for-give-ness of sin. Do this for the re-mem-brance of me.

Gathered into one by the Ho-ly Spir-it, let us pray as Je-sus taught us:

Our Fa-ther in heav-en, hal-lowed be your name,

your king-dom come, your will be done, on earth as in

heav - en. Give us to-day our dai - ly bread.

For - give us our sins as we for-give those who sin a-gainst us.

Save us from the time of tri - al and de-liv-er us from e - vil.

For the king-dom, the pow'r, and the glo-ry are yours,

now and for - ev - er. A - men.

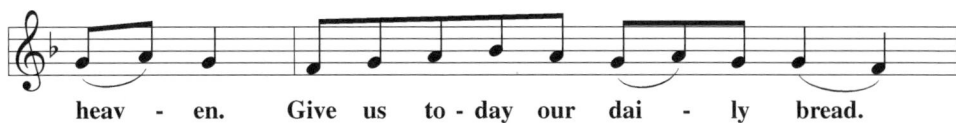

Gathered into one by the Holy Spirit, let us pray as Jesus taught us:

A

Our Father in heaven,
   hallowed be your name,
   your kingdom come,
   your will be done,
      on earth as in heaven.
Give us today our daily bread.
Forgive us our sins
   as we forgive those
      who sin against us.
Save us from the time of trial
   and deliver us from evil.
For the kingdom, the power,
   and the glory are yours,
   now and forever. Amen.

B

Our Father, who art in heaven,
   hallowed be thy name,
   thy kingdom come,
   thy will be done,
      on earth as it is in heaven.
Give us this day our daily bread;
and forgive us our trespasses,
   as we forgive those
      who trespass against us;
and lead us not into temptation,
   but deliver us from evil.
For thine is the kingdom,
   and the power, and the glory,
   forever and ever. Amen.

COMMUNION

The presiding minister may raise the bread and cup and address the assembly with these or similar words:

A

Holy things for holy people.
**One is holy, one is Lord,
Jesus Christ, to the glory of God.**

B

The gifts of God for the people of God.
Thanks be to God.

The assisting minister may conclude the invitation to the meal:
Taste and see that the Lord is good.

The bread may be broken for the communion.

When giving the bread and cup, the communion ministers say:
The body of Christ, given for you. The blood of Christ, shed for you.
and the communicant may respond, Amen.

The ministers commune either after or before the communion of the assembly.

Communion Song
*Assembly song and other music may accompany the breaking of bread and the communion of the people, and
may begin with "Lamb of God".*
R341–R343 ▶

*At the conclusion of the communion, "Now, Lord, you let your servant go" or another appropriate song may be
sung as the table is cleared.*
R344–R346 ▶

Communion Prayer
An assisting minister leads one of these or a similar prayer:
Let us pray.

A

We give you thanks, almighty God,
that you have refreshed us
through the healing power
of this gift of life.
In your mercy
strengthen us through this gift
in faith toward you
and in fervent love toward one another;
for the sake of Jesus Christ our Lord.
Amen.

B

O God, we give you thanks
that you have set before us this feast,
the body and blood of your Son.
By your Spirit
strengthen us to serve all in want
and to give ourselves away
as bread for the hungry,
through Jesus Christ our Lord.
Amen.

SENDING

p. 72 ▸

SENDING OF COMMUNION MINISTERS

Communion ministers may be sent to bring the sacrament to those who are absent. The presiding minister may lead a prayer of sending.

Brief announcements related to the assembly's mission in the world may be made.

BLESSING

The presiding minister blesses the assembly with one of these or another appropriate blessing:

A	*B*	*C*
Holy Eternal Majesty,	The Lord bless you	Almighty God,
Holy Incarnate Word,	and keep you.	Father, ✛ Son,
Holy Abiding Spirit,	The Lord's face shine on	and Holy Spirit,
one God, ✛ bless you	you with grace and mercy.	bless you now and forever.
now and forever.	The Lord look upon you	**Amen.**
Amen.	with favor	
	and ✛ give you peace.	
	Amen.	

SENDING SONG

If "Now, Lord, you let your servant go" was not sung at the end of the communion, it may be sung here, or another sending song may be sung. The ministers may move to the door.

SENDING

The assisting minister sends the assembly forth with these or similar words:

A	*B*	*C*
Go in peace.	Go in peace.	Go in peace.
Share the good news.	Remember the poor.	Serve the Lord.
Thanks be to God.	**Thanks be to God.**	**Thanks be to God.**

HOLY COMMUNION
Provisional Setting B

GATHERING

Instrumental or vocal music or rehearsal of congregational song may take place while the assembly is gathering. An announcement of the day may be made, along with any brief comments about the day's worship.

The remembrance of baptism may precede gathering song. One of the following or another appropriate form may be used. If possible, the ministers (and the assembly) gather at the font.

| I | REMEMBRANCE OF BAPTISM
Confession and Forgiveness

All may make the sign of the cross in remembrance of baptism as the presiding minister begins:

A
Trusting in the word of life
given in baptism,
we are gathered in the name
of the Father, and of the ✝ Son,
and of the Holy Spirit.
Amen.

B
Blessed be God,
who gives us life with all of creation,
joins us to the saving death of ✝ Christ,
and raises us to new life by the Holy Spirit.
Blessed be the Holy Trinity.
Blessed be God forever.

The presiding minister may lead a prayer of preparation:
God of all mercy and consolation,
come to the aid of your people,
turning us from our sin to live for you alone.
Give us the power of your Holy Spirit
that we may confess our sins,
receive your forgiveness,
and grow into the fullness of your Son,
Jesus Christ our Lord.
Amen.

An assisting minister may invite the assembly into the confession:
God so loved the world
that while we were yet sinners
Jesus Christ was given to die for us.
Through the power of the Holy Spirit
God promises to heal us and forgive us.
Let us confess our sin
in the presence of God and of one another.

Silence is kept for reflection and self-examination.

The presiding minister leads a prayer of confession:

A

Gracious God,
**have mercy on us.
In your compassion
forgive us our sins,
known and unknown,
things done and things left undone.
Uphold us by your Spirit
so that we may live and serve you
in newness of life,
to the honor and glory
of your holy name;
through Jesus Christ our Lord.
Amen.**

B

Merciful God,
**we have sinned against you
in thought, word, and deed,
and are not worthy
to be called your children.
Have mercy on us
and turn us from our sinful ways.
Bring us back to you
as those who once were dead
but now have life,
through our Savior Jesus Christ.
Amen.**

The presiding minister announces God's forgiveness:

A

Almighty God looks upon us with mercy
and by water and the word joins us
to the saving death of Jesus Christ.
Through the Holy Spirit
God raises us with Christ to new life.
I therefore declare to you
the entire forgiveness of all your sins,
in the name of the Father,
and of the ☩ Son,
and of the Holy Spirit.
Amen.

B

Almighty God have mercy on you,
forgive you all your sins
through our Lord Jesus Christ,
strengthen you in all goodness,
and by the power of the Holy Spirit
keep you in eternal life.
Amen.

The liturgy may continue with gathering song.

REMEMBRANCE OF BAPTISM
Thanksgiving for Baptism

All may make the sign of the cross in remembrance of baptism as the presiding minister begins:

A

Trusting in the word of life
given in baptism,
we are gathered in the name
of the Father, and of the ✠ Son,
and of the Holy Spirit.
Amen.

B

Blessed be God,
who gives us life with all of creation,
joins us to the saving death of ✠ Christ,
and raises us to new life by the Holy Spirit.
Blessed be the Holy Trinity.
Blessed be God forever.

The assisting minister invites the assembly into the remembrance of baptism:
When we were joined to Christ in the waters of baptism,
we were clothed with God's mercy and forgiveness.
Together let us remember our baptism.

Water may be poured into the font as the presiding minister gives thanks:
The Lord be with you.
And also with you.

Let us give thanks to the Lord our God.
It is right to give our thanks and praise.

We give you thanks, O God,
for in the beginning your Spirit brooded over the waters
and you created the world by your Word,
calling forth life in which you took delight.
You led Israel safely through the Red Sea into the land of promise,
and in the waters of the Jordan, you proclaimed Jesus your beloved one.
By water and the Spirit you adopted us as your daughters and sons,
making us heirs of the promise and servants of God.
Through this water remind us of our baptism.
Shower us with your Spirit,
that your forgiveness, grace, and love may be renewed in our lives.
To you be given honor and praise through Jesus Christ our Lord
in the unity of the Holy Spirit, now and forever.
Amen.

The water may be sprinkled over the people or they may be invited to use it to sign themselves with the cross. During this time gathering song may be sung. Hymns and songs related to baptism are especially appropriate.

The liturgy continues with the greeting and the prayer of the day.

GATHERING SONG

One or more of the following may be sung as the assembly gathers:

Hymn, Song, Psalm

Kyrie
When a Kyrie is sung, one of the following or another appropriate form may be used.

A	Kyrie (Litany)	*R312–R313* ▶
B	Kyrie (Threefold, Sixfold, or Ninefold)	*R314–R317* ▶
C	Holy God (Trisagion)	*R318–R319* ▶

Canticle of Praise
When a canticle of praise is sung, one of the following or another appropriate song may be used.

A	Glory to God	*R320–R322* ▶
B	This is the feast	*R323–R324* ▶

GREETING

The presiding minister and the assembly greet each other:

The grace of our Lord Jesus Christ, the love of God,
and the communion of the Holy Spirit be with you all.
And also with you.

PRAYER OF THE DAY

Let us pray.

A brief silence is kept. Then the presiding minister prays the prayer of the day. The assembly responds:

Amen.

WORD

An announcement of the day may be made, along with any brief comments about the day's liturgy.

FIRST READING

An assisting minister proclaims the reading. The reading may be concluded:

A	B
Holy wisdom, holy word.	The word of the Lord.
Thanks be to God.	**Thanks be to God.**

PSALM *The psalm for the day is sung.*

SECOND READING

An assisting minister proclaims the reading. The reading may be concluded:

A	B
Holy wisdom, holy word.	The word of the Lord.
Thanks be to God.	**Thanks be to God.**

GOSPEL ACCLAMATION

The assembly welcomes the gospel. The verse of the day (R327) or the following verse may be sung. The assembly or the choir may sing another alleluia, with or without verse, in place of this one.

R 306

R325–R329 ▶

Al - le - lu - ia, al - le - lu - ia.

Lord, to whom shall we go? You have the words of e - ter - nal life. Al - le - lu - ia, al - le - lu - ia.

During Lent, the verse of the day, the following verse, or another seasonal acclamation may be sung.

Let your stead-fast love come to us, O Lord;

Save us as you prom-ised, for we trust your word;

save us as you prom-ised, for we trust your word.

GOSPEL

The gospel is announced.

The holy gospel according to _____, the _____ chapter.

Glory to you, O Lord.

The gospel is proclaimed. The reading concludes:

The gospel of the Lord.

Praise to you, O Christ.

SERMON

Silence for reflection follows.

HYMN OF THE DAY

The assembly proclaims the word of God in song.

CREED

The assembly may profess the Nicene Creed or the Apostles Creed. The Nicene Creed is especially appropriate during Christmas, Easter, and on festival days; the Apostles Creed during Lent.

Nicene Creed

We believe in one God,
    the Father, the Almighty,
    maker of heaven and earth,
    of all that is, seen and unseen.

We believe in one Lord, Jesus Christ,
    the only Son of God,
    eternally begotten of the Father,
    God from God, Light from Light,
    true God from true God,
    begotten, not made,
    of one Being with the Father;
    through him all things were made.
    For us and for our salvation
        he came down from heaven,
        was incarnate of the Holy Spirit and the virgin Mary
        and became truly human.
        For our sake he was crucified under Pontius Pilate;
        he suffered death and was buried.
        On the third day he rose again
        in accordance with the scriptures;
        he ascended into heaven
        and is seated at the right hand of the Father.
        He will come again in glory to judge the living and the dead,
        and his kingdom will have no end.

We believe in the Holy Spirit, the Lord, the giver of life,
    who proceeds from the Father and the Son,*
    who with the Father and the Son is worshiped and glorified,
    who has spoken through the prophets.
    We believe in one holy catholic and apostolic church.
    We acknowledge one baptism for the forgiveness of sins.
    We look for the resurrection of the dead,
        and the life of the world to come. Amen.

The phrase "and the Son" does not appear in the ancient, ecumenical version of the creed.

Apostles Creed

I believe in God, the Father almighty,
creator of heaven and earth.

I believe in Jesus Christ, God's only Son, our Lord,
who was conceived by the Holy Spirit,
born of the virgin Mary,
suffered under Pontius Pilate,
was crucified, died, and was buried;
he descended to the dead.
On the third day he rose again;
he ascended into heaven,
he is seated at the right hand of the Father,
and he will come to judge the living and the dead.

I believe in the Holy Spirit,
the holy catholic church,
the communion of saints,
the forgiveness of sins,
the resurrection of the body,
and the life everlasting. Amen.

PRAYERS OF INTERCESSION

The prayers are crafted locally for each occasion using the following pattern or another appropriate form.

An assisting minister invites the assembly into prayer with these or similar words:
With the whole people of God in Christ Jesus, let us pray for the church,
those in need, and all of God's creation.

Prayers reflect the wideness of God's mercy for the whole world:
for the church universal and its ministry;
for creation and its right use;
for peace and justice in the world, the nations and those in authority, the community and those who govern;
for the poor and oppressed, the sick, the bereaved, the lonely, all who suffer in body, mind, or spirit;
for the congregation, and special concerns.

The congregation may be invited to offer other petitions.

The assisting minister gives thanks for the faithful departed, especially for those who recently have died.

Each portion of the prayers concludes with these or similar words:

A	B	p. 56, R331 ▸
Lord, in your mercy,	Hear us, O God;	
hear our prayer.	**your mercy is great.**	

The presiding minister concludes the prayers with these or similar words:

A p. 56 ▸

Into your hands, gracious God, we commend all for whom we pray,
trusting in your mercy; through Jesus Christ our Savior.
Amen.

PEACE

The presiding minister and the assembly greet each other in the peace of the risen Christ:

A

Peace be with you all.

And also with you.

B

The peace of Christ be with you always.

And also with you.

The ministers and the assembly may greet one another with a gesture of Christ's peace, and may say these or similar words: Peace be with you.

MEAL

GATHERING OF GIFTS

Gifts may be gathered for those in need and for the mission of the church.

SETTING THE TABLE

The table of the eucharistic meal is prepared. "Let the vineyards be fruitful" (R332–R333), "Create in me a clean heart" (R334), or another appropriate canticle, song, or hymn may be sung as bread, wine, money, and other gifts are brought to the table. A brief prayer acknowledging God as the source of every gift may follow. pp. 56–57 ▸

GREAT THANKSGIVING

The presiding minister greets the assembly and invites all present to give thanks:

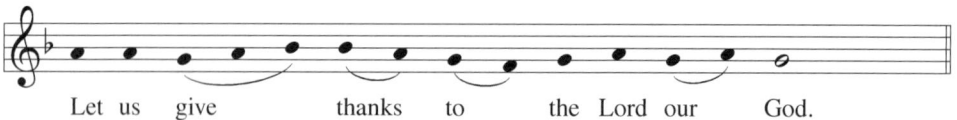

The Lord be with you. **And al - so with you.**

Lift up your hearts. **We lift them to the Lord.**

Let us give thanks to the Lord our God.

It is right to give our thanks and praise.

The presiding minister continues with an initial thanksgiving:

A (Sundays) pp. 57–60 ▶

It is indeed right, our du - ty and our joy, that we should at all times and

in all places give thanks and praise to you, al - mighty and merciful God,

through our Sav - ior Je - sus Christ; who on this day overcame

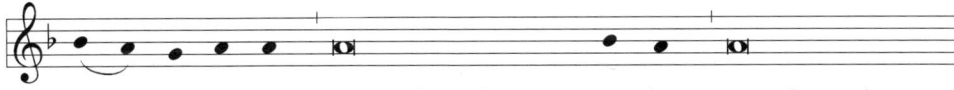

death and the grave, and by his glorious resur - rec - tion opened to us the way

of ev - er - last - ing life. And so, with all the choirs of an - gels,

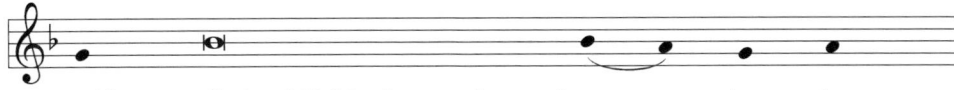

with all the faithful of every time and ev - 'ry place,

we praise your name and join their un - end - ing hymn:

Ho - ly, ho - ly, ho - ly Lord,

God of pow - er and might,

heav - en and earth are full of your glo - ry.

Ho - san - na in the high - est.

Blessed is he who comes in the name of the Lord. Hosanna in the highest, hosanna in the highest.

The presiding minister continues the thanksgiving. One of the following or another appropriate form is used.

A

pp. 61–71 ▶

You are indeed holy, almighty and merciful God.
You are most holy, and great is the majesty of your glory.
You so loved the world that you gave your only Son,
so that everyone who believes in him may not perish
but have eternal life.

Having come into the world to fulfill for us your holy will
and to accomplish all things for our salvation,
in the night in which he was betrayed,
our Lord Jesus took bread, and gave thanks;
broke it, and gave it to his disciples, saying:
Take and eat; this is my body, given for you.
Do this for the remembrance of me.

Again, after supper, he took the cup, gave thanks,
and gave it for all to drink, saying:
This cup is the new covenant in my blood,
shed for you and all people for the forgiveness of sin.
Do this for the remembrance of me.

Remembering, therefore, his salutary command,
his life-giving passion and death,
his glorious resurrection and ascension,
and the promise of his coming again,
we proclaim the mystery of faith.

R 309

R336, R339 ▶

Christ has died. Christ is ris-en. Christ will come a-gain. Christ will come a-gain.

We give thanks to you, O Lord God Almighty,

not as we ought but as we are able;

we ask you mercifully to accept our praise and thanksgiving

and with your Word and Holy Spirit to bless us, your servants,

and these your own gifts of bread and wine,

so that we and all who share in the body and blood of Christ

may be filled with heavenly blessing and grace,

and, receiving the forgiveness of sin,

may be formed to live as your holy people

and be given our inheritance with all your saints.

To you, O God, Father, Son, and Holy Spirit,

be all honor and glory in your holy church, now and forever.

R310
R337, R340 ▶

A - men, a - men, a - men, a - men.

The liturgy continues with the Lord's Prayer on p. 53.

B

In the night in which he was be-trayed, our Lord Je - sus

took bread, and gave thanks; broke it, and gave it to

his dis - ci - ples, say - ing: Take and eat; this is my bod - y,

giv - en for you. Do this for the re - mem - brance of me.

A - gain, after supper, he took the cup, gave thanks, and gave it for all to drink,

say - ing: This cup is the new covenant in my blood, shed for you and all people

for the for - give - ness of sin. Do this for the re - mem - brance of me.

Gathered into one by the Ho - ly Spir - it, let us pray as Je - sus taught us:

Our Fa - ther in heav - en, hal - lowed be your name,

your king - dom come, your will be done, on earth as in

heav - en. Give us to - day our dai - ly bread.

For - give us our sins as we for-give those who sin a-gainst us.

Save us from the time of tri - al and de-liv-er us from e - vil.

For the king - dom, the pow'r, and the glo - ry are yours,

now and for - ev - er. A - men.

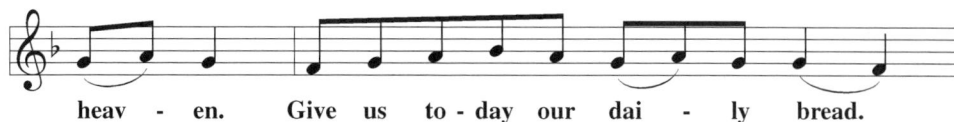

Gathered into one by the Holy Spirit, let us pray as Jesus taught us:

A

Our Father in heaven,
   hallowed be your name,
   your kingdom come,
   your will be done,
      on earth as in heaven.
Give us today our daily bread.
Forgive us our sins
   as we forgive those
      who sin against us.
Save us from the time of trial
   and deliver us from evil.
For the kingdom, the power,
   and the glory are yours,
   now and forever. Amen.

B

Our Father, who art in heaven,
   hallowed be thy name,
   thy kingdom come,
   thy will be done,
      on earth as it is in heaven.
Give us this day our daily bread;
and forgive us our trespasses,
   as we forgive those
      who trespass against us;
and lead us not into temptation,
   but deliver us from evil.
For thine is the kingdom,
   and the power, and the glory,
   forever and ever. Amen.

COMMUNION

The presiding minister may raise the bread and cup and address the assembly with these or similar words:

A

Holy things for holy people.
One is holy, one is Lord,
Jesus Christ, to the glory of God.

B

The gifts of God for the people of God.
Thanks be to God.

The assisting minister may conclude the invitation to the meal:
Taste and see that the Lord is good.

The bread may be broken for the communion.

When giving the bread and cup, the communion ministers say:
The body of Christ, given for you. The blood of Christ, shed for you.
and the communicant may respond, Amen.

The ministers commune either after or before the communion of the assembly.

Communion Song
*Assembly song and other music may accompany the breaking of bread and the communion of the people, and
may begin with "Lamb of God".*   R341–R343 ▶

*At the conclusion of the communion, "Now, Lord, you let your servant go" or another appropriate song may be
sung as the table is cleared.*   R344–R346 ▶

Communion Prayer
An assisting minister leads one of these or a similar prayer:
Let us pray.

A

We give you thanks, almighty God,
that you have refreshed us
through the healing power
of this gift of life.
In your mercy
strengthen us through this gift
in faith toward you
and in fervent love toward one another;
for the sake of Jesus Christ our Lord.
Amen.

B

O God, we give you thanks
that you have set before us this feast,
the body and blood of your Son.
By your Spirit
strengthen us to serve all in want
and to give ourselves away
as bread for the hungry,
through Jesus Christ our Lord.
Amen.

SENDING

SENDING OF COMMUNION MINISTERS

p. 72 ▶

Communion ministers may be sent to bring the sacrament to those who are absent. The presiding minister may lead a prayer of sending.

Brief announcements related to the assembly's mission in the world may be made.

BLESSING

The presiding minister blesses the assembly with one of these or another appropriate blessing:

A	B	C
Holy Eternal Majesty,	The Lord bless you	Almighty God,
Holy Incarnate Word,	and keep you.	Father, ✛ Son,
Holy Abiding Spirit,	The Lord's face shine on	and Holy Spirit,
one God, ✛ bless you	you with grace and mercy.	bless you now and forever.
now and forever.	The Lord look upon you	**Amen.**
Amen.	with favor	
	and ✛ give you peace.	
	Amen.	

SENDING SONG

If "Now, Lord, you let your servant go" was not sung at the end of the communion, it may be sung here, or another sending song may be sung. The ministers may move to the door.

SENDING

The assisting minister sends the assembly forth with these or similar words:

A	B	C
Go in peace.	Go in peace.	Go in peace.
Share the good news.	Remember the poor.	Serve the Lord.
Thanks be to God.	**Thanks be to God.**	**Thanks be to God.**

Supplemental Materials

PRAYERS OF INTERCESSION

Responses

C

Let us pray to the Lord.
Lord, have mercy.

D

God of mercy,
receive our prayer.

Conclusion

B

Holy and eternal God, maker and preserver of all things in heaven and earth:
graciously hear the prayers of your people, and strengthen us to do your will;
through Jesus Christ our Lord.
Amen.

PRAYERS AFTER SETTING THE TABLE

A

Blessed are you, O God,
ruler of heaven and earth.
Day by day you shower us with blessings.
As you have raised us to new life in Christ,
give us glad and generous hearts,
ready to praise you and to respond to those in need;
through Jesus Christ our Savior.
Amen.

B

God of all creation,
all you have made is good,
and your love endures forever.
You bring forth bread from the earth
and fruit from the vine.
Nourish us with these gifts,
that we might be for the world
signs of your gracious presence
in Jesus Christ our Lord.
Amen.

C

God of mercy and grace,
the eyes of all wait upon you,
and you open your hand in blessing.
From all that you have given us, receive these gifts,
signs of our thanksgiving and praise.
Fill us with good things at your table,
that we may come to the help of all in need;
through Jesus Christ, our redeemer.
Amen.

D

Holy God, gracious and merciful,
you bring forth food from the earth
and nourish your whole creation.
Turn our hearts toward those who hunger,
that all may know your care,
and prepare us to feast upon your mercy:
Jesus Christ, the bread of life.
Amen.

INITIAL THANKSGIVINGS

B (Advent)

It is indeed right, our duty and our joy,
that we should at all times and in all places
give thanks and praise to you,
almighty and merciful God.
You comforted your people with the promise of the Redeemer,
through whom you will also make all things new
in the day when he comes to judge the world in righteousness.
And so, with all the choirs of angels,
with all the faithful of every time and every place,
we praise your name and join their unending hymn:

C (Christmas)

It is indeed right, our duty and our joy,
that we should at all times and in all places
give thanks and praise to you,
almighty and merciful God.
In the wonder and mystery of the Word made flesh
you have opened the eyes of faith
to a new and radiant vision of your glory,
that, beholding the God made visible,
we may be drawn to love the God whom we cannot see.
And so, with all the choirs of angels,
with all the faithful of every time and every place,
we praise your name and join their unending hymn:

D (Epiphany/Baptism of the Lord)

A new initial thanksgiving is being developed for these two festivals. The following initial thanksgiving for Transfiguration may be used for these days.

E (Transfiguration)

It is indeed right, our duty and our joy,
that we should at all times and in all places
give thanks and praise to you,
almighty and merciful God.
Sharing our life, Christ lived among us
to reveal your glory and love,
that our darkness should give way to his own brilliant light.
And so, with all the choirs of angels,
with all the faithful of every time and every place,
we praise your name and join their unending hymn:

F (Lent)

It is indeed right, our duty and our joy,
that we should at all times and in all places
give thanks and praise to you,
almighty and merciful God,
through our Savior Jesus Christ.
You call your people to cleanse their hearts
and prepare with joy for the paschal feast,
that, renewed in the waters of baptism,
we may come to the fullness of your grace.
And so, with all the choirs of angels,
with all the faithful of every time and every place,
we praise your name and join their unending hymn:

G (Sunday of the Passion, Holy Week, Maundy Thursday)

It is indeed right, our duty and our joy,
that we should at all times and in all places
give thanks and praise to you,
almighty and merciful God,
through our Savior Jesus Christ,
whose suffering and death gave salvation to all;
for we who were dying, having eaten from the tree,
are restored to life by the tree of the cross.
And so, with all the choirs of angels,
with all the faithful of every time and every place,
we praise your name and join their unending hymn:

H (Vigil and Season of Easter)

It is indeed right, our duty and our joy,

that we should at all times and in all places

give thanks and praise to you,

almighty and merciful God,

for the glorious resurrection of our Lord, Jesus Christ,

the true Paschal Lamb

who gave himself to take away our sin,

who in dying has destroyed death,

and in rising has brought us to eternal life.

And so, with Mary Magdalene and Peter

and all the witnesses of the resurrection,

with earth and sea and all their creatures,

and with angels and archangels, cherubim and seraphim,

we praise your name and join their unending hymn:

I (Ascension)

It is indeed right, our duty and our joy,

that we should at all times and in all places

give thanks and praise to you,

almighty and merciful God,

through our Savior Jesus Christ,

who, enthroned at the right hand of the Father,

intercedes for us as our great high priest.

And so, with all the choirs of angels,

with all the faithful of every time and every place,

we praise your name and join their unending hymn:

J (Vigil and Day of Pentecost)

It is indeed right, our duty and our joy,

that we should at all times and in all places

give thanks and praise to you,

almighty and merciful God.

Fulfilling the promise of the resurrection,

you pour out the fire of your Spirit,

uniting in one body

people of every nation and tongue.

And so, with all the choirs of angels,

with all the faithful of every time and every place,

we praise your name and join their unending hymn:

K (Holy Trinity)

It is indeed right, our duty and our joy,

that we should at all times and in all places

give thanks and praise to you,

almighty and merciful God.

You reveal your glory

as the glory of the Father, the Son, and the Holy Spirit:

equal in majesty, undivided in splendor,
yet one Lord, one God,
ever to be adored in your everlasting glory.
And so, with all the choirs of angels,
with all the faithful of every time and every place,
we praise your name and join their unending hymn:

L (Weekdays)
It is indeed right, our duty and our joy,
that we should at all times and in all places
give thanks and praise to you,
almighty and merciful God,
through our Savior Jesus Christ.
And so, with all the choirs of angels,
with all the faithful of every time and every place,
we praise your name and join their unending hymn:

M (Apostles)
It is indeed right, our duty and our joy,
that we should at all times and in all places
give thanks and praise to you,
almighty and merciful God,
through the great shepherd of your flock, our Savior Jesus Christ;
who after his resurrection sent forth the apostles
to preach the gospel and teach all nations,
and promised to be with them, even to the end of the age.
And so, with _____
and the glorious company of the apostles,
with all the choirs of angels,
with all the faithful of every time and every place,
we praise your name and join their unending hymn:

N (Saints / All Saints)
It is indeed right, our duty and our joy,
that we should at all times and in all places
give thanks and praise to you,
almighty and merciful God,
through our Savior Jesus Christ.
By the witness of the saints
you show us the hope of our calling,
and strengthen us to run the race set before us,
that we may revel in your mercy,
and rejoice with you in glory.
And so, with all the choirs of angels,
with (_____ and) all the faithful of every time and every place,
we praise your name and join their unending hymn:

THANKSGIVINGS AT TABLE

C

Holy God, we praise you.
Let the heavens be joyful,
and the earth be glad.
We bless you for creating the whole world;
for your promises to your people Israel,
and for Jesus Christ in whom your fullness dwells.
Born of Mary, he shares our life.
Eating with sinners, he welcomes us.
Guiding his children, he leads us.
Visiting the sick, he heals us.
Dying on the cross, he saves us.
Risen from the dead, he gives new life.
Living with you, he prays for us.

In the night in which he was betrayed,
our Lord Jesus took bread, and gave thanks;
broke it, and gave it to his disciples, saying:
Take and eat; this is my body, given for you.
Do this for the remembrance of me.

Again, after supper, he took the cup, gave thanks,
and gave it for all to drink, saying:
This cup is the new covenant in my blood,
shed for you and all people for the forgiveness of sin.
Do this for the remembrance of me.

With thanksgiving we take this bread and this cup
and proclaim the mystery of faith.
Christ has died. Christ is risen. Christ will come again.

Pour out your Holy Spirit upon us
that this meal may be
a communion in the body and blood of our Lord.
Make us one with Christ
and with all who share this feast.
Unite us in faith,
encourage us with hope,
inspire us to love,
that we may serve as your faithful disciples
until we feast at your table in glory.

We praise you, eternal God,
through Christ your Word made flesh,
in the holy and life-giving Spirit,
now and forever.
Amen.

Book of Common Worship (Presbyterian Church U.S.A.)

D

This prayer of thanksgiving follows the dialog and includes an initial thanksgiving.

All thanks and praise
are yours at all times and in all places,
our true and loving God,
through Jesus Christ, your eternal Word,
the Wisdom from on high by whom you created all things.
You laid the foundations of the world
and enclosed the sea when it burst out from the womb;
You brought forth all creatures of the earth
and gave breath to humankind.

Wondrous are you, Holy One of Blessing;
all you create is a sign of hope for our journey.
And so as the morning stars sing your praises
we join the heavenly beings and all creation as we shout with joy:

Holy, holy, holy Lord,
God of power and might,
heaven and earth are full of your glory.
Hosanna in the highest.
Blessed is he who comes in the name of the Lord.
Hosanna in the highest.

Glory and honor are yours, Creator of all,
your Word has never been silent;
you called a people to yourself, as a light to the nations,
you delivered them from bondage
and led them to a land of promise.
Of your grace, you gave Jesus
to be human, to share our life,
to proclaim the coming of your holy reign
and give himself for us, a fragrant offering.

Through Jesus Christ our redeemer,
you have freed us from sin,
brought us into your life,
reconciled us to you,
and restored us to the glory you intend for us.

In the night in which he was betrayed,
our Lord Jesus took bread, and gave thanks;
broke it, and gave it to his disciples, saying:
Take and eat; this is my body, given for you.
Do this for the remembrance of me.

Again, after supper, he took the cup, gave thanks,
and gave it for all to drink, saying:
This cup is the new covenant in my blood,
shed for you and all people for the forgiveness of sin.
Do this for the remembrance of me.

And so, remembering all that was done for us—
the cross, the tomb, the resurrection and ascension—
longing for Christ's coming in glory,
and presenting to you these gifts
your earth has formed and human hands have made,
we proclaim the mystery of faith:
Christ has died. Christ is risen. Christ will come again.

Send your Holy Spirit upon us
and upon these gifts of bread and wine
that they may be to us
the body and blood of your Christ.
Grant that we, burning with your Spirit's power,
may be a people of hope, justice, and love.

Giver of life, draw us together in the body of Christ,
and in the fullness of time gather us
with (blessed _____, and) all your people
into the joy of our true eternal home.

Through Christ and with Christ and in Christ,
by the inspiration of your Holy Spirit,
we worship you, our God and Creator,
in voices of unending praise, now and forever.
Amen.

Enriching Our Worship (The Episcopal Church)

This prayer of thanksgiving follows the dialog and includes an initial thanksgiving.

Holy God, Holy One, Holy Three!
Before all that is, you were God.
Outside all we know, you are God.
After all is finished, you will be God.
Archangels sound the trumpets,
angels teach us their song,
saints pull us into your presence.

And this is our song:
Holy, holy, holy Lord,
God of power and might,
heaven and earth are full of your glory.
Hosanna in the highest.
Blessed is he who comes in the name of the Lord.
Hosanna in the highest.

Holy God, Holy One, Holy Three!
You beyond the galaxies,
you under the oceans,
you inside the leaves,
you pouring down rain,
you opening the flowers,
you feeding the insects,
you giving us your image,
you carrying us through the waters,
you holding us in the night;
your smile on Sarah and Abraham,
your hand with Moses and Miriam,
your words through Deborah and Isaiah—
you lived as Jesus among us,
healing, teaching, dying, rising,
inviting us all to your feast.

In the night in which he was betrayed,
our Lord Jesus took bread, and gave thanks;
broke it, and gave it to his disciples, saying:
Take and eat; this is my body, given for you.
Do this for the remembrance of me.

Again, after supper, he took the cup, gave thanks,
and gave it for all to drink, saying:
This cup is the new covenant in my blood,
shed for you and all people for the forgiveness of sin.
Do this for the remembrance of me.

Holy God, we remember your Son,
his life with the humble,
his death among the wretched,
his resurrection for us all:
your wisdom our guide,
your justice our strength,
your grace our path to rebirth.

And so we cry, Mercy:
Mercy!
And so we cry, Glory:
Glory!
And so we cry, Blessing:
Blessing!

Holy God, we beg for your Spirit.
Enliven this bread,
awaken this body,
pour us out for each other.
Transfigure our minds,
ignite your church,
nourish the life of the earth.
Make us, while many, united;
make us, though broken, whole;
make us, despite death, alive.

And so we cry, Come, Holy Spirit:
Come, Holy Spirit!
And so the church shouts, Come, Holy Spirit:
Come, Holy Spirit!
And so the earth pleads, Come, Holy Spirit:
Come, Holy Spirit!

You, Holy God, Holy One, Holy Three—
our Life, our Mercy, our Might,
our Table, our Food, our Server,
our Rainbow, our Ark, our Dove,
our Sovereign, our Water, our Wine,
our Light, our Treasure, our Tree,
our Way, our Truth, our Life—
You, Holy God, Holy One, Holy Three!

Praise now,
praise tomorrow,
praise forever!
And so we cry, Amen:
Amen!

Celebrate God's Presence (United Church of Canada)

O God most mighty,
O God most merciful,
O God, our rock and our salvation,
hear us as we praise,
call us to your meal,
grant to us your life.

When everything was in chaos, you formed beauty and order.
When Abraham and Sarah were childless, you birthed them a son.
When the Israelites were enslaved, you led them to freedom.
David faced Goliath and the widow of Zarephath drought,
Naaman leprosy and Esther the slaughter of her people,
and the stories proclaim that you granted them all your life.

To our world of sorrow you came as Jesus our brother.
He was born into poverty, he lived under oppression,
he wept at Lazarus' tomb.

In the night in which he was betrayed,
our Lord Jesus took bread, and gave thanks;
broke it, and gave it to his disciples, saying:
Take and eat; this is my body, given for you.
Do this for the remembrance of me.

Again, after supper, he took the cup, gave thanks,
and gave it for all to drink, saying:
This cup is the new covenant in my blood,
shed for you and all people for the forgiveness of sin.
Do this for the remembrance of me.

We remember his death, and let the people say, Amen.
Amen.
We celebrate his resurrection, and let the people shout, Amen.
Amen.
We beg him to come again and again, and let the people plead, Amen.
Amen.

O God, you are Bread: may we live by this food.
O God, you are Breath: may your Spirit enliven our bones.
O God, you are Fire: may your church illumine the world.
O God, you are Fortress: may there be no more war.
O God, you are Harvest: may there be no more hunger.
O God, you are Light: may no one die alone or in despair.

From your throne teach us justice,
in your sheepfold give us protection,
in your arms may we find peace.
O God most majestic,
O God most motherly,
grant to us your life,
life as of the Father to the Son,
life as of the Spirit of our risen Lord,
life as of a tree bearing twelve different fruits, now and forever.
Amen.

G

Holy God,
you alone are holy,
you alone are God.

The universe declares your praise:
beyond the stars,
beneath the sea,
within each cell,
with every breath.
We praise you, O God.

Generations bless your faithfulness;
through the water,
by night and day,
across the wilderness,
out of exile,
into the future.
We bless you, O God.

We give you thanks for your Son:
at the heart of human life,
near to those who suffer,
beside the sinner,
among the poor,
with us now.
We thank you, O God.

In the night in which he was betrayed,
our Lord Jesus took bread, and gave thanks;
broke it, and gave it to his disciples, saying:
Take and eat; this is my body, given for you.
Do this for the remembrance of me.

Again, after supper, he took the cup, gave thanks,
and gave it for all to drink, saying:
This cup is the new covenant in my blood,
shed for you and all people for the forgiveness of sin.
Do this for the remembrance of me.

Remembering his love for us
on the way, at the table, and to the end,
we proclaim the mystery of faith:
Christ has died. Christ is risen. Christ will come again.

We pray for the gift of your Spirit
in our gathering,
upon this bread,
within this cup,
among your people,
throughout the world.

Blessing, praise, and thanks to you,
holy God,
for your mercy,
through Christ Jesus,
by your Spirit,
in your church,
without end.
Amen.

H

God of our weary years, God of our silent tears,
you have brought us this far along the way.
In times of bitterness you did not abandon us,
but guided us into the path of love and light.
In every age you sent prophets
to make known your loving will for all humanity.
The cry of the poor has become your own cry;
our hunger and thirst for justice is your own desire.
In the fullness of time, you sent your chosen servant
to preach good news to the afflicted,
to break bread with the outcast and despised,
and to ransom those in bondage to prejudice and sin.

In the night in which he was betrayed,
our Lord Jesus took bread, and gave thanks;
broke it, and gave it to his disciples, saying:
Take and eat; this is my body, given for you.
Do this for the remembrance of me.
Again, after supper, he took the cup, gave thanks,
and gave it for all to drink, saying:
This cup is the new covenant in my blood,
shed for you and all people for the forgiveness of sin.
Do this for the remembrance of me.

For as often as we eat of this bread and drink from this cup
we proclaim the Lord's death until he comes.
Christ has died. Christ is risen. Christ will come again.

Remembering, therefore, his death and resurrection,
we await the day when Jesus shall return to free all the earth
from the bonds of slavery and death.
Come, Lord Jesus! And let the church say, Amen.
Amen.

Send your Holy Spirit, our advocate,
to fill the hearts of all who share this bread and cup
with courage and wisdom to pursue love and justice in all the world.
Come, Spirit of freedom! And let the church say, Amen.
Amen.

Join our prayers and praise with your prophets and martyrs of every age,
that, rejoicing in the hope of the resurrection,
we might live in the freedom and hope of your Son,
through whom, and with whom, and in whom,
in the unity of the Holy Spirit,
all glory and honor is yours, almighty Father,
now and forever.
Amen.

⏐ A Guide to Giving Thanks at the Table

The thanksgiving is introduced with the following dialog or with a simple invitation to prayer.

The Lord be with you.
And also with you.
Lift up your hearts.
We lift them to the Lord.
Let us give thanks to the Lord our God.
It is right to give our thanks and praise.

The presiding minister begins with praise for our salvation and redemption, possibly referring to a theme suggested by the season or festival. These sentences may conclude with a vision of the church in all times and places united in singing God's praise. This is particularly helpful as a cue to "Holy, holy, holy":

Holy, holy, holy Lord,
God of power and might,
heaven and earth are full of your glory.
Hosanna in the highest.
Blessed is he who comes in the name of the Lord.
Hosanna in the highest.

The minister continues the prayer by citing the reason for our praise, recalling God's love, faithfulness, and grace
    as shown in creation
    as experienced by the people of ancient Israel
    as revealed to us in the saving work of Jesus Christ.
OR
If a brief prayer is appropriate, the minister recalls the saving purpose of God's revelation in Christ.

The minister proclaims the words of institution:
In the night in which he was betrayed,
our Lord Jesus took bread, and gave thanks;
broke it, and gave it to his disciples, saying:
Take and eat; this is my body, given for you.
Do this for the remembrance of me.

Again, after supper, he took the cup, gave thanks,
and gave it for all to drink, saying:
This cup is the new covenant in my blood,
shed for you and for all people for the forgiveness of sin.
Do this for the remembrance of me.

The minister remembers the life, death, and resurrection of Jesus, praying that the salvation always present in Jesus may now be present and active among us.
The minister prays for the transforming, renewing, and healing power of the Holy Spirit in this sacrament.
The minister concludes the prayer by praising the glory of the triune God.
The assembly says Yes to the prayer of thanksgiving by speaking or singing: **Amen.**

All pray together the Lord's Prayer.

SENDING OF COMMUNION MINISTERS

A

Gracious God,
loving all your family with a mother's tender care:
As you sent the angel to feed Elijah with heavenly bread,
assist those who set forth from this assembly
to share your word and sacrament
with those who are sick and homebound.
In your love and care,
nourish and strengthen those to whom we bring this sacrament,
that through the body and blood of your Son
we all may know the comfort of your abiding presence.
Amen.

B

Compassionate God,
as Jesus called disciples to follow him,
bless those who go forth
to share your word and sacrament
with the sick and homebound of our congregation.
May they be signs of our love and prayers,
that through the sharing of the body and blood of Christ,
all may know your grace and healing
revealed in Jesus Christ our Lord.
Amen.

C

Eternal God,
whose glory is revealed in the crucified and risen Lord:
bless those who go forth to share your word and sacrament
with our absent sisters and brothers.
In your love and care, nourish and strengthen those
to whom we bring this communion
in the body and blood of your Son,
that we may all feast upon your abundant love
made known in Jesus Christ our Lord.
Amen.

Models for Shaping the Liturgy
Examples for Various Seasons and Contexts

The shape of the rite for the services in *Holy Communion and Related Rites* allows for considerable flexibility across the seasons of the church's year and in a variety of contexts. The examples that follow offer a few illustrations of how the options and supplemental materials in this volume, as well as other suggested resources, may be used in a variety of circumstances.

See the Renewing Worship Web site at www.renewingworship.org for additional suggestions and for downloadable text and music files suitable for building worship folders with these rites.

Example One — Advent

As is the case with all of the examples in this volume, this outline is intended to give one illustration of how the elements of the liturgy might be arranged during this season rather than to prescribe a normative practice.

GATHERING

Remembrance of Baptism I — Confession and Forgiveness
Gathering Song
   Hymn, Song, or Psalm
   Kyrie — Litany
Greeting
Prayer of the Day

WORD

First Reading
Psalm
Second Reading
Gospel Acclamation — Verse of the Day (see Renewing Worship, vol. 8)
    or "Lord, to whom shall we go"
Gospel
Sermon
Hymn of the Day
Nicene Creed
Prayers of Intercession
Peace

MEAL

Gathering of Gifts
Setting the Table — "Let the vineyards be fruitful" or another appropriate song
Great Thanksgiving
    Dialog and Thanksgiving — Initial Thanksgiving B for Advent (p. 57)
       or A for Sundays (p. 14)
    Holy, Holy, Holy
    Thanksgiving — Prayer D (pp. 62–63), *WOV* Prayer A, or another
    Lord's Prayer
Communion
    Communion Song
    Communion Prayer — Communion Prayer B

SENDING

Sending of Communion Ministers (optional)
Blessing — Blessing C
Sending — Sending B

Example Two — Nativity of the Lord

As is the case with all of the examples in this volume, this outline is intended to give one illustration of how the elements of the liturgy might be arranged during this season rather than to prescribe a normative practice.

GATHERING

Gathering Song
    Hymns and songs of the season
    Canticle of Praise — "Glory to God"
Greeting
Prayer of the Day

WORD

First Reading
Psalm
Second Reading
Gospel Acclamation — Verse of the Day (see Renewing Worship, vol. 8), a hymn such as
    "Let our gladness have no end" (LBW 57), or "Lord, to whom shall we go"
Gospel
Sermon
Hymn of the Day
Nicene Creed
Prayers of Intercession
Peace

MEAL

Gathering of Gifts
Setting the Table — "Let the vineyards be fruitful" or another appropriate song
Great Thanksgiving
    Dialog and Thanksgiving — Initial Thanksgiving C for Christmas (p. 57)
    Holy, Holy, Holy
    Thanksgiving — Prayer A, *WOV* Prayer IV or B, or another
    Lord's Prayer
Communion
    Communion Song — ending with "Now, Lord, you let your servant go"
    Communion Prayer — Communion Prayer A

SENDING

Sending of Communion Ministers (optional)
Blessing — Blessing A
Sending Song
Sending — Sending C

Example Three — Epiphany of the Lord and Baptism of the Lord

As is the case with all of the examples in this volume, this outline is intended to give one illustration of how the elements of the liturgy might be arranged on these days rather than to prescribe a normative practice.

GATHERING

Remembrance of Baptism II — Thanksgiving for Baptism
Gathering Song
    Baptism Hymn, Song, or Psalm
    Canticle of Praise — "Glory to God"
Greeting
Prayer of the Day

WORD

First Reading
Psalm
Second Reading
Gospel Acclamation — Verse of the Day (see Renewing Worship, vol. 8)
      or "Your words are sweet"
Gospel
Sermon
Hymn of the Day
Nicene Creed
Prayers of Intercession
Peace

MEAL

Gathering of Gifts
Setting the Table — "Let the vineyards be fruitful" or another appropriate song
Great Thanksgiving
    Dialog and Thanksgiving — Initial Thanksgiving D for Epiphany/Baptism of the Lord
      (p. 58)
    Holy, Holy, Holy
    Thanksgiving — Prayer C (page 61), *WOV* Prayer C, or another
    Lord's Prayer
Communion
    Communion Song
    Communion Prayer — Communion Prayer A

SENDING

Sending of Communion Ministers (optional)
Blessing — Blessing B
Sending Song — "Now, Lord, you let your servant go"
Sending — Sending A

Example Four — Lent

As is the case with all of the examples in this volume, this outline is intended to give one illustration of how the elements of the liturgy might be arranged during this season rather than to prescribe a normative practice.

GATHERING

Remembrance of Baptism I — Confession and Forgiveness
Gathering Song
    Kyrie — Litany or other Kyrie
Greeting
Prayer of the Day

WORD

First Reading
Psalm
Second Reading
Gospel Acclamation — Verse of the Day (see Renewing Worship, vol. 8)
      or "Let your steadfast love"
Gospel
Sermon
Hymn of the Day
Apostles Creed
Prayers of Intercession
Peace

MEAL

Gathering of Gifts
Setting the Table — "Let the vineyards be fruitful" or another appropriate song
Great Thanksgiving
    Dialog and Thanksgiving — Initial Thanksgiving F for Lent (p. 58)
      or A for Sundays (p. 14)
    Holy, Holy, Holy
    Thanksgiving — Prayer F (pp. 66–67), *WOV* Prayer D, or another
    Lord's Prayer
Communion
    Communion Song, beginning with "Lamb of God"
    Communion Prayer — Communion Prayer B

SENDING

Sending of Communion Ministers (optional)
Blessing — Blessing B
Sending Song — "Now, Lord, you let your servant go"
Sending — Sending A

Example Five — Easter

As is the case with all of the examples in this volume, this outline is intended to give one illustration of how the elements of the liturgy might be arranged during this season rather than to prescribe a normative practice.

GATHERING

Remembrance of Baptism II — Thanksgiving for Baptism
Gathering Song
    Hymn or Song
    Litany — Holy God (Trisagion)
    Canticle of Praise — This is the feast
Greeting
Prayer of the Day

WORD

First Reading
Psalm
Second Reading
Gospel Acclamation — Verse of the Day (see Renewing Worship, vol. 8)
    or "Lord, to whom shall we go"
Gospel
Sermon
Hymn of the Day
Nicene Creed
Prayers of Intercession
Peace

MEAL

Gathering of Gifts
Setting the Table — "Let the vineyards be fruitful" or another appropriate song
Great Thanksgiving
    Dialog and Thanksgiving — Initial Thanksgiving H for Easter (p. 59)
    Holy, Holy, Holy
    Thanksgiving — Prayer E (pp. 64–65), *WOV* Prayer E (F for Pentecost), or another
    Lord's Prayer
Communion
    Communion Song, ending with "Now, Lord, you let your servant go"
    Communion Prayer — Communion Prayer A

SENDING

Sending of Communion Ministers (optional)
Blessing — Blessing C
Sending Song
Sending — Sending C

Example Six — *Time after Epiphany, Time after Pentecost*

As is the case with all of the examples in this volume, this outline is intended to give one illustration of how the elements of the liturgy might be arranged during these times, rather than to prescribe a normative practice.

GATHERING

Remembrance of Baptism I — Confession and Forgiveness
Gathering Song
   Hymn, song, or psalm (one or more)
Greeting
Prayer of the Day

WORD

First Reading
Psalm
Second Reading
Gospel Acclamation — Verse of the Day (see Renewing Worship, vol. 8),
   "Lord, to whom shall we go, " or "Your words are sweet"
Gospel
Sermon
Hymn of the Day
Apostles Creed
Prayers of Intercession
Peace

MEAL

Gathering of Gifts
Setting the Table — "Let the vineyards be fruitful" or another appropriate song
Great Thanksgiving
   Dialog and Thanksgiving — Initial Thanksgiving A for Sundays (p. 14)
   Holy, Holy, Holy
   Thanksgiving — Prayer G (pp. 68–69), A, or another
   Lord's Prayer
Communion
   Communion Song
   Communion Prayer

SENDING

Sending of Communion Ministers (optional)
Blessing — Blessing C
Sending — Sending A

Example Seven — Time after Pentecost (November)

As is the case with all of the examples in this volume, this outline is intended to give one illustration of how the elements of the liturgy might be arranged during this time rather than to prescribe a normative practice.

GATHERING

Remembrance of Baptism II — Thanksgiving for Baptism
Gathering Song
    Hymn, song, or psalm (one or more)
    Canticle of Praise — "This is the feast"
Greeting
Prayer of the Day

WORD

First Reading
Psalm
Second Reading
Gospel Acclamation — Verse of the Day (see Renewing Worship, vol. 8)
      or "Your words are sweet"
Gospel
Sermon
Hymn of the Day
Apostles Creed
Prayers of Intercession
Peace

MEAL

Gathering of Gifts
Setting the Table — "Let the vineyards be fruitful" or another appropriate song
Great Thanksgiving
    Dialog and Thanksgiving — Initial Thanksgiving A for Sundays (p. 14)
    Holy, Holy, Holy
    Thanksgiving — Prayer H (p. 70), *WOV* Prayer IV or I (November), or another
    Lord's Prayer
Communion
    Communion Song, ending with "Now, Lord, you let your servant go"
    Communion Prayer — Communion Prayer B

SENDING

Sending of Communion Ministers (optional)
Blessing — Blessing A
Sending — Sending B

Example Eight — Informal Worship with a Praise Team

As is the case with all of the examples in this volume, this outline is intended to give one illustration of how the elements of the liturgy might be arranged for such a setting rather than to prescribe a normative practice.

GATHERING

Gathering Song
   Songs and psalms
Greeting
Prayer of the Day

WORD

First Reading
Psalm (may be done in paraphrase set to music)
Second Reading
Gospel Acclamation — "Your words are sweet" or "Lord, to whom shall we go"
Gospel
Sermon
Hymn of the Day
Apostles Creed (optional)
Prayers of Intercession
Peace

MEAL

Gathering of Gifts
Setting the Table — "Let the vineyards be fruitful" or another appropriate song
Great Thanksgiving
   Crafted locally, using "A Guide to Giving Thanks at the Table" (p. 71)
   Lord's Prayer
Communion
   Communion Song
   Communion Prayer — Communion Prayer B

SENDING

Sending of Communion Ministers (optional)
Blessing — Blessing B
Sending Song
Sending

Example Nine — A Festive Occasion

As is the case with all of the examples in this volume, this outline is intended to give one illustration of how the elements of the liturgy might be arranged for such an occassion rather than to prescribe a normative practice.

Points in the liturgy that are especially appropriate for choral or instrumental embellishment include gathering song, psalm, gospel acclamation, hymn of the day, gathering of gifts, and communion song.

GATHERING

Remembrance of Baptism II — Thanksgiving for Baptism
Gathering Song
    Hymns or Songs
    Holy God (Trisagion)
    Canticle of Praise — "Glory to God"
Greeting
Prayer of the Day

WORD

First Reading
Psalm
Second Reading
Gospel Acclamation — Verse of the Day (see Renewing Worship, vol. 8)
    or "Your words are sweet"
Gospel
Sermon
Hymn of the Day
Nicene Creed
Prayers of Intercession
Peace

MEAL

Gathering of Gifts
Setting the Table — "Let the vineyards be fruitful" or another appropriate song
Great Thanksgiving
    Dialog and Thanksgiving — Initial Thanksgiving A for Sundays (p. 14)
      or another appropriate one
    Holy, Holy, Holy
    Thanksgiving — Prayer A or another
    Lord's Prayer
Communion
    Communion Song
Communion Prayer — Communion Prayer B

SENDING

Sending of Communion Ministers (optional)
Blessing — Blessing A
Sending Song
Sending — Sending C

Example Ten — Weekday Liturgy with a Small Group

As is the case with all of the examples in this volume, this outline is intended to give one illustration of how the elements of the liturgy might be arranged for such a setting rather than to prescribe a normative practice.

GATHERING

Gathering Song
   Psalm, hymn, or song
Greeting
Prayer of the Day

WORD

First Reading
Psalm (optional)
Second Reading (optional — either the appointed first reading or second reading may be used)
Gospel
Sermon (may take an informal style)
Hymn of the Day
Prayers of Intercession
Peace

MEAL

Gathering of Gifts — or gifts may be gathered as people leave
Setting the Table
Great Thanksgiving
   Dialog and Thanksgiving — Initial Thanksgiving L for weekdays (p. 60)
   Holy, Holy, Holy
   Thanksgiving — Prayer B or another
   Lord's Prayer
Communion
   Communion Song (optional)
   Communion Prayer — Communion Prayer B

SENDING

Blessing — Blessing C
Sending — Sending C

Word and Thanksgiving

Shape of the Rite

GATHERING	*The Holy Spirit gathers us in unity.*

WORD	*God speaks to us in scriptures read, sung, and preached.*

THANKSGIVING	*God's grace and mercy summons us to give thanks.*

Hymn or Prayer	*We begin our thanksgiving with words sung or spoken.*
Gathering of Gifts	*We gather gifts for those in need and the church's mission.*
Thanksgiving for the Word	*We remember God's deeds of love and give thanks for them.*
Lord's Prayer	*Empowered by the Spirit, we are bold to pray the prayer Jesus taught.*

SENDING	*God blesses us and sends us in mission to the world.*

Blessing	*God blesses us and sends us in mission to the world.*
Sending Song	*Singing, we go out from the assembly as God's people in mission.*
Sending	*We bless the Lord and give thanks in word and deed.*

Central elements of the liturgy are noted in bold letters; other elements support and reveal the essential shape of Christian worship.

WORD and THANKSGIVING

Word and Thanksgiving is a pattern for worship on those occasions when the liturgy does not include the Lord's supper. After the gathering and word sections from Holy Communion (pp. 6–14, 19–28, or 38–46), the liturgy may be concluded with the thanksgiving and sending sections that follow here.

GATHERING

WORD

THANKSGIVING

GATHERING OF GIFTS

A hymn of praise and thanksgiving may be sung during or after the gathering of gifts.

THANKSGIVING FOR THE WORD

The following or a similar prayer of thanksgiving is said or sung:
The Lord be with you.
And also with you.

Let us give thanks to the Lord our God.
It is right to give our thanks and praise.

Praise and thanks to you, holy God,
for by your Word you made all things:
You spoke light into darkness,
called forth beauty from chaos,
and brought life into being.
Praise and thanks to you, holy God,
for your Word of life.

By your Word you called a people
to tell of your wonderful deeds:
freedom from captivity,
water on the desert journey,
a pathway home from exile.
Praise and thanks to you, holy God,
for your Word of life.

Mindful of your covenant,
you spoke of old by the prophets:
words of warning and of woe,
words to challenge and console,
wisdom for our life with you.
Praise and thanks to you, holy God,
for your Word of life.

Now you call to us through Jesus,
your Word made flesh among us:
light for those who dwell in darkness,
life to those entombed by death,
the way of your self-giving love.
Praise and thanks to you, holy God,
for your Word of life.

Send your Spirit of truth, O God;
rekindle your gifts within us:
renew our faith,
increase our hope,
and deepen our love
for the sake of a world in need.

Be faithful to your word, O God;
draw near to those who call on you:
lift up the weak and lowly;
bring justice to the hungry;
guide us in the ways of peace,
for you alone are God,
to you alone we sing our praise:

The assembly sings this canticle of praise or another appropriate song:

R311

Sal - va - tion be - longs to our God and to Christ the Lamb for -

ev-er and ev - er. Great and won-der-ful are your deeds, O

God of the u - ni - verse; just and true are your ways, O

Rul-er of all the na - tions. Who can fail to hon-or you, Lord, and

sing the glo - ry of your name? Sal - va-tion be-longs to our

God and to Christ the Lamb for - ev - er and ev - er.

For you a - lone are the Ho - ly One, and

bless - ed is the one whose name is the Word of

God. All praise and thanks to you, ho - ly God!

Salvation belongs to our God and to Christ the Lamb forever and ever.

Gathered into one by the Holy Spirit, let us pray as Jesus taught us:

A

Our Father in heaven,
    hallowed be your name,
    your kingdom come,
    your will be done,
        on earth as in heaven.
Give us today our daily bread.
Forgive us our sins
    as we forgive those
        who sin against us.
Save us from the time of trial
    and deliver us from evil.
For the kingdom, the power,
    and the glory are yours,
        now and forever. Amen.

B

Our Father, who art in heaven,
    hallowed be thy name,
    thy kingdom come,
    thy will be done,
        on earth as it is in heaven.
Give us this day our daily bread;
and forgive us our trespasses,
    as we forgive those
        who trespass against us;
and lead us not into temptation,
    but deliver us from evil.
For thine is the kingdom,
    and the power, and the glory,
        forever and ever. Amen.

SENDING

Brief announcements related to the assembly's mission in the world may be made.

BLESSING

The presiding minister blesses the assembly:
Go forth into the world to serve God with gladness;
be of good courage;
hold fast to that which is good;
render to no one evil for evil;
strengthen the fainthearted;
support the weak;
help the afflicted;
honor all people;
love and serve God,
rejoicing in the power of the Holy Spirit.

A
Almighty God,
Father, ✝ Son,
and Holy Spirit,
bless you now and forever.
Amen.

B
The Lord bless you and keep you.
The Lord's face shine on you
with grace and mercy.
The Lord look upon you with favor
and ✝ give you peace.
Amen.

SENDING SONG

A sending hymn or song may be sung.

SENDING

The assisting minister may send the assembly forth:
Let us bless the Lord.
Thanks be to God.

Service Music

Litany

In peace, let us pray to the Lord.

Lord, have mer - cy.

For the peace from a-bove, and for our sal-vation, let us pray to the Lord.

Lord, have mer - cy.

*Sing the lower note or the upper notes

Leader: For the peace of the whole world, for the well-being of the church of God, and for the unity of all, let us pray to the Lord.

Assembly: Lord, have mer-cy.

Leader: For this ho-ly house, and for all who offer here their wor-ship and praise, let us pray to the Lord. **Lord, have mer-cy.**

Help, save, comfort, and de-fend us, gra-cious Lord.

A - men.

Music: Joel Martinson

Litany

Leader

In peace, let us pray to the Lord.

Assembly

Lord, have mer - cy.

Leader

For the peace from a - bove, and for

our sal - va - tion, let us pray to the Lord.

Assembly

Lord, have mer - cy.

Leader

For the peace of the whole world, for the well - be - ing of the church of God, and for the u - ni - ty of all, let us pray to the Lord.

Assembly

Lord, have mer - cy.

Leader

For this ho-ly house, and for all who of-fer here their

wor-ship and praise, let us pray to the Lord.

Assembly

Lord, have mer-cy.

Leader

Help, save, com-fort, and de-

fend us, gra-cious Lord.

Assembly

A - men.

Music: Marty Haugen

Ninefold

Lord, have mer - cy, Lord, have mer - cy,

Lord, have mer - cy.

Christ, have mer - cy, Christ have mer - cy,

Music: Joel Martinson

R315 Kyrie

Nkosi, Nkosi

Lord, have mer - cy; have mer - cy up - on us.
Nko - si, Nko - si, yi - ba nen - ce - ba.

Christ, have mer - cy; have mer - cy up - on us.
Kres - tu, Kres - tu, yi - ba nen - ce - ba.

Lord, have mer - cy; have mer - cy up - on us.
Nko - si, Nko - si, yi - ba nen - ce - ba.

Music: G. M. Kolisi
Music © 1984 Utryck, admin. Walton Music Corporation. Used by permission.
You must contact Walton Music Corporation at 305/563-1844 for permission to reproduce this selection.

R 316 Kyrie

Lord, have mercy

Lord, have mer - cy,

Christ, have mer - cy,

Lord, have mer - cy on us.

Repeat as desired

Last time

* Accompaniment may be played an octave lower.

Music: Swee Hong Lim

Music © General Board of Global Ministries, GBGMusik. Used by permission.

You must contact GBGMusik at 475 Riverside Dr., Room 350, New York, NY 10115 for permission to reproduce this selection.

R 317 Kyrie

Sixfold

Leader | Assembly

Lord, have mer - cy. **Lord, have mer - cy.**

Leader | Assembly

Christ, have mer - cy. **Christ, have mer - cy.**

Leader | Assembly

Lord, have mer - cy. **Lord, have mer - cy.**

Music: Traditional plainsong

R 318 Holy God

Trisagion

Ho - ly, ho - ly, ho - ly God, ho - ly and might - y,

ho - ly and im - mor - tal, have mer - cy on us.

Music: Traditional Russian Orthodox

Trisagion

Ho - ly God,   ho - ly and might - y,

ho - ly and im - mor - tal,   have mer - cy on us.

Music: Mark Mummert

Glo - ry to God in the high - est, and

peace to God's peo-ple on   earth.   **Glo - ry to God in the**

high - est, and   peace to God's peo-ple on   earth.

Lord God, heav'n-ly king, al - might-y God and Fa - ther; we wor-ship you, we give you thanks, we praise you for your glo - ry. Glo - ry to God in the high - est, and peace to God's peo-ple on earth.

Lord Je-sus Christ, on-ly Son of the
Fa-ther, Lord God, Lamb of God; you
take a-way the sin of the world: have
mer-cy on us; you are

seat-ed at the right hand of the Fa-ther: re-ceive our prayer. Glo-ry to God in the high - est, and peace to God's peo-ple on earth.

For you a - lone are the Ho - ly One, you a -

lone are the Lord, you a - lone are the

Most High, Je - sus Christ, with the Ho - ly

Spir - it, in the glo - ry of God the Fa - ther.

A - men,

a - men.

Music: Joel Martinson

Glo-ry to God in the high-est, and peace to God's peo-ple on earth. Glo-ry to God in the high-est, and peace to God's peo-ple on earth. Lord God, heav-en-ly King, al-might-y God and

Fa - ther, we wor - ship you, we give you thanks, we praise you for your glo - ry.

Glo - ry to God in the high - est, and peace to God's peo - ple on earth. Glo - ry to God in the high - est, and peace to God's peo - ple on earth.

Lord Je - sus Christ, on - ly Son of the Fa - ther,

Lord God, Lamb of God, you take a - way the

sin of the world: have mer - cy on us; you are

seat - ed at the right hand of the Fa - ther: re - ceive our prayer.

Glo-ry to God in the high-est, and peace to God's peo-ple on earth. Glo-ry to God in the high - est, and peace to God's peo - ple on earth.

For you a - lone are the Ho - ly One,

you a - lone are the Lord, you a - lone are the

Most High, Je - sus Christ, with the Ho - ly Spir-it, in the glo-ry of God the Fa - ther. A - men.

Glo-ry to God in the high-est, and peace to God's peo-ple on earth. Glo-ry to God in the high-est, and peace to God's peo-ple on earth.

Music: Marty Haugen

Glo-ry to God in the high-est, and peace to God's peo-ple on earth.

Lord God, heav-en-ly King, al-might-y God and Fa-ther,

we wor-ship you, we give you thanks, we praise you for your glo-ry.

Lord Je-sus Christ, on-ly Son of the Fa-ther,

Lord God, Lamb of God, you take a-way the sin of the world:

have mer-cy on us; you are seat-ed at the right hand of the Fa-ther:

re-ceive our prayer. For you a-lone are the Ho-ly One,

you a-lone are the Lord, you a-lone are the Most High,

Je-sus Christ, with the Ho-ly Spir-it,

in the glo-ry of God the Fa-ther. A-men.

Music: David Hurd
Music © 1980 GIA Publications, Inc. All rights reserved. Used by permission.
You must contact GIA Publications at 800/GIA-1358 for permission to reproduce this selection.

This is the feast of vic-to-ry for our God.

Al-le-lu - ia, al-le-lu - ia.

Wor-thy is Christ, the Lamb who was slain, whose

blood set us free to be peo-ple of God.

Pow - er, rich - es, wis - dom and strength, and hon - or, bless - ing and glo - ry are his.

This is the feast of vic - to - ry for our God.

Al - le - lu - ia, al - le - lu - ia.

Sing with all the peo-ple of God, and join in the hymn of all cre - a - tion: Bless - ing, hon - or, glo - ry and might be to God and the Lamb for-ev - er. A - men. This is the feast of

vic-to-ry for our God, for the Lamb who was
slain has be-gun his reign. Al-le-lu-ia,
al-le-lu-ia, al-le-lu-ia.

Text: John Arthur
Music: Joel Martinson
Text © 1978 *Lutheran Book of Worship*, admin. Augsburg Fortress
Music © 2004 Augsburg Fortress. All rights reserved.

This is the feast of vic - to - ry for our God. Al - le - lu - ia, al - le - lu - ia, al - le - lu - ia.

Wor-thy is Christ, the Lamb who was slain, whose blood set us free to be peo-ple of God. Pow-er, rich-es, wis-dom and strength, and hon-or, bless-ing, and glo-ry are his.

This is the feast of vic-to-ry for our God. Al-le-lu-ia, al-le-lu-ia, al-le-lu-ia. Sing with all the peo-ple of God, and join in the hymn of all cre - a - tion:

Bless - ing, hon - or, glo - ry and might be to

God and the Lamb for - ev - er. A - men.

This is the feast of vic - to - ry for our God,

for the Lamb who was slain has be - gun
his reign. Al - le - lu - ia,
al - le - lu - ia, al - le - lu - ia.

Text: John Arthur
Music: Marty Haugen

Verse of the day

Al - le - lu - ia, al - le - lu - ia.

Al - le - lu - ia, al - le - lu - ia.

Verse (cantor or choir)

Music: Joel Martinson

Lord, to whom shall we go?

Al - le - lu - ia, al - le - lu - ia.

Al - le - lu - ia, al - le - lu - ia.

Lord, to whom shall we go?

You have the words of e - ter - nal life. Al - le - lu - ia. Al - le - lu - ia, al - le - lu - ia. Al - le - lu - ia, al - le - lu - ia.

Music: Joel Martinson

Verse of the day

Al - le - lu - ia, al - le - lu - ia.

Al - le - lu - ia.

Verse (cantor or choir)

Al - le - lu - ia, al - le - lu - ia.

Music: Marty Haugen

Your words are sweet

Al - le - lu - ia, al - le - lu - ia,

al - le - lu - ia. Your

words are sweet to our taste, sweet - er than

honey to our mouth. Al - le - lu - ia, al - le - lu - ia.

Music: Marty Haugen

R 329   Alleluia

Al - le - lu - ia,   al - le - lu - ia,   al - le - lu - ia.

Fine

Al - le - lu - ia,   al - le - lu - ia,   al - le - lu - ia.

Verse (cantor or choir)   *   *D.C. al Fine*

Al - le - lu - ia!

D.C. al Fine

(hum)

* Choose either part.

Music: Alleluia 7, Jacques Berthier and the Taizé Community
Music © 1984 Les Presses de Taizé, admin. GIA Publications, Inc. Used by permission.
You must contact GIA Publications at 800/GIA-1358 for permission to reproduce this selection.

R 330   Lenten Acclamation

Verse (cantor or choir)

Glo-ry to you, O Word of God, Lord Je - sus Christ.

Music: Richard Proulx

R 331   Response to Intercessions

O Lord, hear our prayer

Text and music: Ralph C. Sappington

Text and music © 1999 Augsburg Fortress. All rights reserved.

Let the vine-yards be fruit-ful, Lord, and

fill to the brim our cup of bless - ing.

Gath-er a har-vest from the seeds that were sown, that

we may be fed with the bread of life.

Gath-er the hopes and dreams of all; u - nite them with the prayers we of - fer. Grace our ta - ble with your pres - ence, and give us a fore - taste of the feast to come.

Text: John Arthur
Music: Joel Martinson
Text © 1978 *Lutheran Book of Worship*, admin. Augsburg Fortress
Music © 2004 Augsburg Fortress. All rights reserved.

Let the vine-yards be fruit-ful, Lord, and

fill to the brim our cup of bless-ing.

Gath-er a har-vest from the seeds that were sown, that

we may be fed with the bread of life.

Gath-er the hopes and the dreams of all, u-nite them with the prayers we of-fer. Grace our ta-ble with your pres-ence, and give us a fore-taste of the feast to come.

Text: John Arthur
Music: Marty Haugen
Text © 1978 *Lutheran Book of Worship,* admin. Augsburg Fortress
Music © 2004 Augsburg Fortress. All rights reserved.

Create in me a clean heart, O God, and re-
new a right spir-it with-in me.
Cast me not a-way from your pres-ence, and take not your
Ho-ly Spir-it from me. Re-

store to me the joy of your sal - va - tion, and up -

hold me with your free Spir - it.

Cre - ate in me a clean heart, O God, and re -

new a right spir - it with - in me.

Music: James Capers, *Liturgy of Joy*; arr. Dennis Friesen-Carper, *This Far by Faith*

Holy, ho - ly, ho - ly Lord, God of pow - er and might, heav - en and earth are full of your glo - ry. Ho - san - na in the high - est. Bless - ed is he who comes in the name of the Lord. Ho - san - na in the high - est, ho - san - na in the high - est.

Music: Per Harling

R 336 Acclamation

Christ has died. Christ is ris - en. Christ will come a - gain.

Music: Per Harling

R 337 Amen

A - men, a - men, a - men.

Music: Per Harling

Ho-ly, ho-ly, ho-ly Lord, God of pow-er and might,

heav'n and earth are full of your glo-ry. Ho-

san-na in the high-est, ho-san-na in the high-est.

Blest is he who comes in the name of the Lord. Ho-san - na in the high - est, ho - san-na in the high-est.

R 339 Acclamation

Christ has died. Christ is ris - en. Christ will come a - gain.

R 340 Amen

A - men, a - men, a - men.

Lamb of God, you take a - way the sin of the

world; have mer - cy on us.

Lamb of God, you take a - way the sin of the

world; have mer-cy on us. Lamb of God, you

take a-way the sin of the world; grant us

peace, grant us peace.

Music: Joel Martinson

Lamb of God,   you take a - way the sin   of the

world; have mer - cy on us.   Lamb of God,   you

take a - way the sin   of the   world;   have mer - cy on us. Lamb of God, you

take a-way the sin of the world; grant us peace.

Music: Marty Haugen

R 343 Lamb of God
Cordero de Dios

Spanish: Cor-de-ro de Dios, tú que qui-tas el pe-ca-do del mun-do: ten pie-dad de no-so-tros, ten pie-dad de no-so-tros. Cor-de-ro de Dios, tú que qui-tas el pe-ca-do del mun-do: ten pie-dad de no-so-tros, ten pie-dad de no-so-tros. Cor-de-ro de Dios, tú que qui-tas el pe-ca-do del mun-do: Da-nos tu paz, da-nos tu paz.

English: O Lamb of God, you take a-way the sin of the world: have mer-cy up-on us, have mer-cy up-on us. O Lamb of God, you take a-way the sin of the world: have mer-cy up-on us, have mer-cy up-on us. O Lamb of God, you take a-way the sin of the world: Grant us your peace, grant us your peace.

Music: Victor Jortack, *Libro de Liturgia y Cántico*
Music © 1998 Augsburg Fortress

Now, Lord, you let your ser - vant go in peace: your word has been ful - filled. My own eyes have seen the sal - va - tion which you have pre - pared in the sight of ev - 'ry peo - ple: a light to re - veal you to the

na - tions and the glo - ry of your peo - ple

Is - ra - el. Glo - ry to the Fa - ther, and

to the Son, and to the Ho-ly Spir - it,
as it was in the be - gin - ning, is
now, and will be for - ev - er. A -
men, a - men, a - men.

Music: Joel Martinson
Music © 2004 Augsburg Fortress. All rights reserved.

R 345   Now, Lord, you let your servant go   Provisional Setting B

Now, Lord, you let your ser-vant go in peace: your

word has been ful-filled. My own eyes have seen the sal-

va-tion which you have pre-pared in the sight of ev-'ry

peo - ple: a light to re - veal you to the

na - tions and the glo - ry of your peo - ple Is - ra - el.

Glo - ry to the Fa - ther, and to the Son, and to the Ho - ly

Spir - it: as it was in the be - gin - ning, is now, and will be for - ev - er. A - men.

Music: Marty Haugen

Now, Lord,   you let your servant go in peace: your word has been ful-filled.

My own eyes have seen the sal-va-tion   which you have prepared in the sight of

ev - 'ry peo - ple: a   light   to reveal you to the na - tions

and the glory of your   peo - ple   Is - ra - el.

Glo - ry   to the Father, and to the Son,   and to the Ho - ly Spir - it:

as it was in the beginning, is now,   and will be for - ev - er.   A - men.

Music: Traditional plainsong

Acknowledgments

Holy Communion and Related Rites editorial team: Karen Bockelman, Susan Briehl, James Brown, Robert Buckley Farlee, Gordon Lathrop; Michael Burk, Cheryl Dieter, Martin A. Seltz (Renewing Worship project management staff).

Liturgical Music editorial team: Kevin Anderson, Teresa Bowers, Lorraine Brugh, David Cherwien, Thomas Pavlechko, Scott Weidler; Michael Burk, Cheryl Dieter, Martin A. Seltz (Renewing Worship project management staff).

Holy Communion and Related Rites development panel: Michael Aune, Mark Bangert, Lorraine Brugh, Joseph Donnella II, Franz Volker Greifenhagen, Robert Hawkins, Susan Hedahl, Walter Huffman, Dirk Lange, Henry Langknecht, Timothy Lull [†], Harry Maier, Rafael Malpica-Padilla, Melissa Maxwell-Dougherty, Ruth Meyers, George Murphy, James Nieman, Mark Oldenburg, Michael Pryse, Melinda Quivik, Thomas Ridenhour, Robert Rimbo, Michael Rogness, Lester Ruth, Craig Satterlee, Thomas H. Schattauer, Frank Senn, S. Anita Stauffer, Karen Walhof.

Design and production: Jessica Hillstrom, Becky Lowe, Mark Weiler, production; Carolyn Porter of The Kantor Group, Inc., book design; Nicholas Markell, logo design.

The material on pages i—169 is covered by the copyright of this book. Unless otherwise noted, the material has been prepared by the editorial team. Material from the sources listed here is gratefully acknowledged and is used by permission. Every effort has been made to identify the copyright administrators for copyrighted texts and music. The publisher regrets any oversight that may have occurred and will make proper acknowledgment in future editions if correct information is brought to the publisher's attention.

Scripture quotations, unless otherwise noted, are from the New Revised Standard Version Bible © 1989 Division of Christian Education of the National Council of Churches of Christ in the United States of America. Used by permission.

Book of Common Prayer (1979) of The Episcopal Church: declaration of forgiveness B, 7, 20, 39; conclusion to prayers of intercession B, 56

Book of Common Worship of the Presbyterian Church (U.S.A.), © 1993 Westminster John Knox Press: thanksgiving at table C, 61

Celebrate God's Presence, The United Church of Canada: thanksgiving at table E, 64–65, © 2000 Gail Ramshaw

Commissioned music prepared by Per Harling, © 2004 Augsburg Fortress: R335 "Holy, holy, holy," R336 "Acclamation," R337 "Amen"

Commissioned music prepared by Marty Haugen, © 2004 Augsburg Fortress: R306 "Alleluia," R307 "Lenten Acclamation," R308 "Holy, holy, holy," R309 "Acclamation,"

R310 "Amen," R313 "Kyrie," R321 "Glory to God," R324 "This is the feast," R327 "Alleluia," R328 "Alleluia," R333 "Let the vineyards be fruitful," R342 "Lamb of God," R345 "Now, Lord, you let your servant go"

Commissioned music prepared by Joel Martinson, © 2004 Augsburg Fortress: R301 "Alleluia," R302 "Lenten Acclamation," R303 "Holy, holy, holy," R304 "Acclamation," R305 "Amen," R312 "Kyrie," R314 "Kyrie," R320 "Glory to God," R323 "This is the feast," R325 "Alleluia," R326 "Alleluia," R332 "Let the vineyards be fruitful," R341 "Lamb of God," R344 "Now, Lord, you let your servant go"

Commissioned music prepared by Mark Mummert, © 2003 Augsburg Fortress: R319 "Holy God"

Commissioned text prepared by Gail Ramshaw, © 2004 Augsburg Fortress: thanksgiving at table F, 66–67

Enriching Our Worship 1: Morning and Evening Prayer, The Great Litany, The Holy Eucharist, © 1998 The Church Pension Fund: blessing A, 18, 37, 55; thanksgiving at table D, 62–63

Holy Baptism and Related Rites, Renewing Worship, vol. 3, © 2002 admin. Augsburg Fortress: invitation into the confession, 6, 19, 38; prayer of confession B, 7, 20, 39

Lutheran Book of Worship and *Lutheran Book of Worship* Ministers Edition © 1978 Lutheran Church in America, The American Lutheran Church, The Evangelical Lutheran Church of Canada, and The Lutheran Church—Missouri Synod: Kyrie litany A, 9; initial thanksgivings (prefaces), 14, 29, 47, 57–60; thanksgiving at table A, B, 15–16, 32–34, 50–52; texts of "This is the feast," 10, R323–R324, and "Let the vineyards be fruitful," R332–R333

Occasional Services, © 1982 Association of Evangelical Lutheran Churches, Lutheran Church in America, The American Lutheran Church, The Evangelical Lutheran Church of Canada: sending of communion ministers A, 72

Praying Together, © 1988 English Language Liturgical Consultation (ELLC): texts of Apostles Creed, Nicene Creed, great thanksgiving dialog, Lord's Prayer, "Glory to God," "Holy, holy, holy," "Lamb of God," "Now, Lord, you let your servant go"

Service music: see service music section for acknowledgments

Sundays and Seasons 1996-1997, © 1996 Augsburg Fortress: setting the table B, 56; *Sundays and Seasons 1997-1998,* © 1997 Augsburg Fortress: sending of communion ministers B, C, 72; *Sundays and Seasons 1999,* © 1998 Augsburg Fortress: blessing B, 18, 37, 55, setting the table C, 51; *Sundays and Seasons 2002,* © 2001 Augsburg Fortress: setting the table A, 56

Evaluation

An essential goal of Renewing Worship is the use and evaluation of trial-use resources by worshiping communities and their leaders. Such feedback will help shape decisions on final resources. Included here as well as at www.renewingworship.org is a reproducible evaluation tool that can be used to evaluate the rites and music contained in *Holy Communion and Related Rites*.

This evaluation form is separated into two parts, which will allow you to evaluate either the rites (shape and texts of the liturgies) or the music, or both. Because of the amount of material included in this volume, you may wish to submit multiple evaluations, identifying smaller sections in your review. Be sure to include the completed last page of the evaluation with each submission.

Please use check marks to identify the material you are evaluating:

RITES (Questions 1-9 below):

HOLY COMMUNION
_____ Entire rite
    OR
_____ Gathering
_____ Word
_____ Meal
_____ Sending

SUPPLEMENTAL MATERIALS
_____ Prayers of Intercession
_____ Setting the Table
_____ Initial Thanksgivings
_____ Thanksgivings at Table
_____ Sending of Communion Ministers

SERVICE OF WORD AND THANKSGIVING
_____ Entire rite (Gathering and Word same as Holy Communion rite)
    OR
_____ Thanksgiving
_____ Sending

MUSIC (Questions 10-17 below):

Holy Communion: Provisional Settings *(choose one)*
_____ Provisional Setting A
_____ Provisional Setting B
Service music section R312–R346. Please identify the specific piece of liturgical music you are evaluating: R _____

Please indicate your agreement with the statements that follow by circling the appropriate number. If desired, add comments to support your response.

RITES

1. The rite is faithful to scripture and the church's tradition.

Agree   Disagree
1   2   3   4   5
Comments:

2. The style and language of the rite are accessible to our worshiping assembly.

Agree   Disagree
1   2   3   4   5
Comments:

3. The rite is easy to follow and to adapt for our worshiping assembly.

Agree   Disagree
1   2   3   4   5
Comments:

4. The shape of the rite is a helpful guide to the flow and the flexibility of the liturgy.

Agree   Disagree
1   2   3   4   5
Comments:

5. Who was involved in the planning related to use of this rite?

_____ Pastor(s)
_____ Pastor(s) and musicians
_____ Pastor(s), musicians, and other staff
_____ Group of lay members with pastoral and other staff
_____ Other (describe): _____

6. In what context was the rite used?

_____ As a regularly scheduled service
_____ Outside of a regularly scheduled service
_____ Studied but not used in worship
_____ Other (describe): _____

7. How many times did you use the rite prior to this evaluation? _____

8. One of the goals of Renewing Worship is to provide options that can be used in flexible ways. Which statement best describes the options provided in this rite?

_____ A sufficient number of options are provided with the rite.
_____ Too many options are provided with the rite.
_____ Too few options are provided with the rite.

9. Please note any additional comments and suggestions:

If you are not evaluating the music of the rite, please skip questions 10 through 17 and complete the information at the end of the evaluation form.

MUSIC

10. The text and the music are well-matched.

Agree				Disagree
1	2	3	4	5

Comments:

11. The music invites the assembly's active participation.

Agree				Disagree
1	2	3	4	5

Comments:

12. The melody is appropriate for congregational singing.

Agree				Disagree
1	2	3	4	5

Comments:

13. The accompaniment provided is accessible to our music leader(s).

Agree				Disagree
1	2	3	4	5

Comments:

14. What type of accompaniment was used to support the singing of the music? (Select all that apply).

_____ Organ
_____ Piano/keyboard
_____ Guitar(s)
_____ Drum(s)
_____ Orchestra (strings and/or wind instruments)
_____ Band and/or praise band
_____ Other (please specify): _____

15. How many times did you use the music prior to this evaluation? _____ —

16. In your opinion, should this music be included in (select one answer only):

_____ A primary common resource
_____ Secondary, supplemental materials
_____ Not necessary to include

17. Please note any additional comments or suggestions about the music:

ISBN 0-8066-7006-1

90000